THIRD EDITION

Python
Pocket Reference

Mark Lutz

Beijing · Cambridge · Farnham · Köln · Paris · Sebastopol · Taipei · Tokyo

Python Pocket Reference
by Mark Lutz

Copyright © 2005, 2002, 1998 O'Reilly Media, Inc. All rights reserved.
Printed in the United States of America.

Published by O'Reilly Media, Inc., 1005 Gravenstein Highway North,
Sebastopol, CA 95472.

O'Reilly books may be purchased for educational, business, or sales
promotional use. Online editions are also available for most titles
(*safari.oreilly.com*). For more information, contact our corporate/
institutional sales department: (800) 998-9938 or *corporate@oreilly.com*.

Editor:	Jonathan Gennick
Production Editor:	Claire Cloutier
Cover Designer:	Edie Freedman
Interior Designer:	David Futato

Printing History:

October 1998:	First Edition.
January 2002:	Second Edition.
February 2005:	Third Edition.

0-596-00940-2
[C]

Contents

Python Pocket Reference

Introduction

Python is a general-purpose, object-oriented, and open source computer programming language. It is commonly used for both standalone programs and scripting applications in a wide variety of domains, by hundreds of thousands of developers.

Python is designed to optimize developer productivity, software quality, program portability, and component integration. Python programs run on most platforms in common use, including mainframes and supercomputers, Unix and Linux, Windows and Macintosh, Palm OS and Pocket PC, Java and .NET, and more.

This pocket reference summarizes Python statements and types, built-in functions, commonly used library modules, and other prominent Python tools. It is intended to serve as a concise reference tool for developers and is designed to be a companion to other books that provide tutorials, code examples, and other learning materials.

This third edition covers Python Version 2.4 and later. It has been thoroughly updated for recent language and library changes and expanded for new topics. Most of it applies to earlier releases as well, with the exception of recent language extensions.

Conventions

The following conventions are used in this book:

[ ]

    Items in brackets are usually optional. The exceptions are those cases where brackets are part of Python's syntax.

*

    Something followed by an asterisk can be repeated zero or more times.

a | b

    Items separated by a bar are often alternatives.

Italic

    Used for filenames and URLs and to highlight new terms.

`Constant width`

    Used for code, commands, and command-line options, and to indicate the names of modules, functions, attributes, variables, and methods.

`Constant width italic`

    Used for replaceable parameter names in command syntax.

Command-Line Options

```
python [option*]
  [ scriptfilename | -c command | -m module | - ] [arg*]
```

Python Options

`-d`

    Turns on parser debugging output (for developers of the Python core).

`-E`

    Ignores environment variables (such as `PYTHONPATH`).

`-h`

   Prints help message and exit.

`-i`

   Enters interactive mode after executing a script, without reading the PYTHONSTARTUP file. Useful for postmortem debugging.

`-O`

   Optimizes generated byte-code (create and use *.pyo* byte-code files). Currently yields a minor performance improvement.

`-OO`

   Operates like -O, the previous option, but also removes docstrings from byte-code.

`-Q arg`

   Division options: -Qold (default), -Qwarn, -Qwarnall, -Qnew.

`-S`

   Doesn't imply "import site" on initialization.

`-t`

   Issues warnings about inconsistent tab usage (-tt issues error instead).

`-u`

   Forces *stdout* and *stderr* to be unbuffered and binary.

`-v`

   Prints a message each time a module is initialized, showing the place from which it is loaded; repeats this flag for more verbose output.

`-V`

   Prints Python version number and exit.

-W *arg*

Functions as warning control; arg is *action*:*message*: *category*:*module*:*lineno*. See warnings module documentation in the Python Library Reference (*http://www. python.org/doc/*).

-x

Skips first line of source, allowing use of non-Unix forms of #!cmd.

Program Specification

scriptfilename

Denotes the name of a Python scriptfile to execute; the main, topmost file of a program, made available in sys.argv[0].

-c *command*

Specifies a Python command (as a string) to execute; sys.argv[0] is set to -c.

-m *module*

Runs library module as a script: searches for module on sys.path, and runs it as a top-level file (e.g., python -m profile runs the Python profiler).

-

Reads Python commands from *stdin* (the default); enters interactive mode if *stdin* is a tty (interactive device).

*arg**

Indicates that anything else on the command line is passed to the scriptfile or command (and appears in the built-in list of strings sys.argv[1:]).

If no *scriptfilename*, *command*, or *module* is given, Python enters interactive mode, reading commands from *stdin* (and using GNU readline, if installed, for input).

Besides using traditional command lines, you can also generally start Python programs by clicking their filenames in a file explorer GUI, by calling functions in the Python/C API, by using program launch menu options in IDEs such as IDLE and Komodo, and so on.

Environment Variables

PYTHONPATH
> Augments the default search path for imported module files. The format is the same as the shell's PATH setting: directory pathnames separated by colons (semicolons on DOS). On module imports, Python searches for the corresponding file or directory in each listed directory, from left to right. Merged into sys.path.

PYTHONSTARTUP
> If set to the name of a readable file, the Python commands in that file are executed before the first prompt is displayed in interactive mode.

PYTHONHOME
> If set, the value is used as an alternate prefix directory for library modules (or sys.prefix, sys.exec_prefix). The default module search path uses sys.prefix/lib.

PYTHONCASEOK
> If set, ignores case in import statements (on Windows).

PYTHONDEBUG
> If nonempty, same as -d option.

PYTHONINSPECT
> If nonempty, same as -i option.

PYTHONOPTIMIZE
> If nonempty, same as -O option.

PYTHONUNBUFFERED
> If nonempty, same as -u option.

PYTHONVERBOSE
> If nonempty, same as -v option.

Built-in Types and Operators

Operators and Precedence

Table 1 lists Python's expression operators. Operators in the lower cells of this table have higher precedence (i.e., bind tighter) when used in mixed-operator expressions without parentheses.

Table 1. Expression operators and precedence

Operator	Description
`lambda args: expr`	Anonymous function maker.
`X or Y`	Logical OR: Y is evaluated only if X is false.
`X and Y`	Logical AND: Y is evaluated only if X is true.
`not X`	Logical negation.

`X < Y, X <= Y, X > Y, X >= Y`
`X == Y, X <> Y, X != Y`
`X is Y, X is not Y`
`X in S, X not in S`
	Comparison operators[a].
	Equality operators.
	Object identity tests.
	Sequence membership.

`X | Y`	Bitwise OR.
`X ^ Y`	Bitwise exclusive OR.
`X & Y`	Bitwise AND.
`X << Y, X >> Y`	Shift X left, right by Y bits.
`X + Y, X – Y`	Addition/concatenation, subtraction.
`X * Y, X % Y, X / Y, X // Y`	Multiply/repetition, remainder/format, division, floor division[b].
`-X, +X, ~X, X ** Y`	Unary negation, identity, bitwise complement, power.
`X[i], X[i:j], X.attr, X(...)`	Indexing, slicing, attribute references, function calls.
`(...), [...], {...}, `...``	Tuple[c], list[d], dictionary, conversion to string[e].

[a] Comparison operators can be chained: x < y < z is similar to x < y and y < z, except that y is evaluated only once in the first format.

[b] *Floor* division (X // Y), new in Python Version 2.2, always truncates fractional remainders. *Classic* division (X / Y) truncates integer division results in Version 2.2 but will be changed to *true* division (always keeping remainders) in Version 3.0. In Version 2.2 and later, use from __future__ import division to make the / operator return a true division result (e.g., 1/2 is 0.5).

[c] In Python 2.4, expressions in parentheses can also be generator expressions, which are similar to list comprehensions but produce a series of values on demand in iteration contexts.

[d] List literals in square brackets ([. . .]) can be a simple list of expressions, or a list comprehension; see the later section "List comprehension expressions."

[e] String conversion expressions return the as-code display of an object, and are equivalent to calling the built-in repr function; the built-in str function provides an alternative user-friendly conversion.

Operations by Category

All built-in types support the comparisons and Boolean operations listed in Table 2.

Boolean true means any nonzero number or any nonempty collection object (list, dictionary, etc.). The names True and False are pre-assigned to true and false values and behave like integers 1 and 0. The special object None is false.

Comparisons return True or False and are applied recursively in compound objects as needed to determine a result.

Boolean and and or operators stop (short-circuit) as soon as a result is known and return one of the two operand objects (on left or right).

Table 2. Comparisons and Boolean operations

Operator	Description
X < Y	Strictly less than[a]
X <= Y	Less than or equal to
X > Y	Strictly greater than
X >= Y	Greater than or equal to
X == Y	Equal to (same value)
X != Y	Not equal to (same as X < >Y)[b]

Table 2. Comparisons and Boolean operations (continued)

Operator	Description
X is Y	Same object
X is not Y	Negated object identity
X < Y < Z	Chained comparisons
not X	If X is false then True; else, False
X or Y	If X is false then Y; else, X
X and Y	If X is false then X; else, Y

[a] For comparison expression overloading, see both the rich comparison (e.g., __lt__ for <) and general __cmp__ class methods in the section "Operator Overloading Methods," later in this book.
[b] != and <> both mean not equal by value, but != is the preferred syntax. is performs an identity test; == performs value comparison.

Tables 3 through 6 define operations common to types in the three major type categories (sequence, mapping, and number), as well as operations available for mutable (changeable) types in Python. Most types also export additional type-specific operations (e.g., methods), as described in the section "Specific Built-in Types," later in this book.

Table 3. Sequence operations (strings, lists, and tuples)

Operation	Description	Class method
X in S X not in S	Membership tests	__contains__, __iter__, __getitem__ [a]
for X in S:	Iteration	__getitem__, __iter__
S + S	Concatenation	__add__
S * N, N * S	Repetition	__mul__
S[i]	Index by offset	__getitem__
S[i:j]	Slicing	__getslice__, __getitem__ [b]
len(S)	Length	__len__
iter(S)	Iterator object	__iter__
min(S)	Minimum item	__getitem__
max(S)	Maximum item	__getitem__

Table 4. Mutable sequence operations (lists)

Operation	Description	Class method
S[i] = X	Index assignment: change item at existing offset i.	__setitem__
S[i:j] = S2, S[i:j:k] = S2	Slice assignment: S from i to j is replaced by S2, with optional stride k.	__setslice__, __setitem__
del S[i]	Index deletion.	__delitem__
del S[i:j], del S[i:j:k]	Slice deletion.	__delslice__, __delitem__

Table 5. Mapping operations (dictionaries)

Operation	Description	Class method
D[k]	Index by key.	__getitem__
D[k] = X	Key assignment: change or create entry for key k.	__setitem__
del D[k]	Delete item by key.	__delitem__
len(D)	Length (number of keys).	__len__
k in D	Same as D.has_key(k).	Same as in Table 3
k not in D	Converse of k in D.	Same as in Table 3
for k in D:	Iterate through keys in D.	Same as in Table 3

Table 6. Numeric operations (all number types)

Operation	Description	Class method
X + Y, X - Y	Add, subtract.	__add__, __sub__
X * Y, X / Y, X % Y	Multiply, divide, remainder.	__mul__, __div__, __mod__
-X, +X	Negative, identity.	__neg__, __pos__
X | Y, X & Y, X ^ Y	Bitwise OR, AND, exclusive OR (integers).	__or__, __and__, __xor__

Table 6. Numeric operations (all number types) (continued)

Operation	Description	Class method
X << N, X >> N	Bitwise left-shift, right-shift (integers).	__lshift__, __rshift__
~X	Bitwise invert (integers).	__invert__
X ** Y	X to the power Y.	__pow__
abs(X)	Absolute value.	__abs__
int(X)	Convert to integer.	__int__
long(X)	Convert to long.	__long__
float(X)	Convert to float.	__float__
complex(X), complex(re,im)	Make a complex value.	__complex__
divmod(X, Y)	Tuple: (X/Y, X%Y).	__divmod__
pow(X, Y [,Z])	Raise to a power.	__pow__

Sequence Operation Notes

Indexing: S[i]

- Fetches components at offsets (first item is at offset 0).
- Negative indexes mean to count backward from the end.
- S[0] fetches the first item.
- S[-2] fetches the second-to-last item (S[len(S) - 2]).

Slicing: S[i:j]

- Extracts contiguous sections of a sequence.
- Slice boundaries default to 0 and sequence length.
- S[1:3] fetches from offsets 1 up to, but not including, 3.
- S[1:] fetches from offsets 1 through the end (length-1).
- S[:-1] fetches from offsets 0 up to, but not including, the last item.
- S[:] makes a top-level (shallow) copy of sequence object S.
- Slice assignment is similar to deleting and then inserting.

Slicing: S[i:j:k]

- If present, the third item k is a stride: added to the offset of each item extracted.
- S[::2] is every other item in sequence S.
- S[::-1] is sequence S reversed.
- S[4:1:-1] fetches from offsets 4 up to, but not including, 1, reversed.

Other

- Concatenation, repetition, and slicing return new objects (not always for tuples).

Specific Built-in Types

This section covers numbers, strings, lists, dictionaries, tuples, files, and other built-in types. Compound datatypes (e.g., lists, dictionaries, and tuples) can nest inside each other arbitrarily, and as deeply as required.

Numbers

This section covers basic number types (integers, floating-point), as well as more advanced types (complex, unlimited-precision long integers). Numbers are always immutable (unchangeable).

Literals

Numbers are written in a variety of numeric constant forms.

1234, -24, 0
Normal integers (C longs, at least 32 bits)

99999999L, 42l
Long integers (unlimited size)

1.23, 3.14e-10, 4E210,.4.0e+210, 1., .1
Floating-point (C doubles)

```
0177, 0x9ff
```
   Octal and hex integer constants

```
3+4j, 3.0+4.0j, 3J
```
   Complex numbers

Operations

Number types support all number operations (see Table 6, earlier in this book). In mixed-type expressions, Python converts operands up to the type of the "highest" type, where integer is lower than long, which is lower than floating-point, which is lower than complex.

In Version 2.2 and later, integer results are automatically promoted to longs instead of overflowing, so there is no need to manually code an integer with a trailing letter "L" to force long precision. Also, in Version 2.2 and later, there are two flavors of division (/ and //).

Strings

Strings are immutable (i.e., unchangeable) arrays of characters, accessed by offset.

Literals

Strings are written as a series of characters in quotes.

```
"Python's", 'Python"s'
```
   Double and single quotes work the same, and each can embed unescaped quotes of the other kind.

```
"""This is a
   multiline block"""
```
   Triple-quoted blocks collect lines into a single string, with end-of-line markers (\n) inserted between the original lines.

`'Python\'s\n'`

> Backslash escape code sequences (see Table 7) are replaced with the special-character byte values they represent (e.g., `'\n'` is a byte with binary value 012).

`"This" "is" "concatenated"`

> Adjacent string constants are concatenated.

`r'a raw\string', R'another\one'`

> Raw strings: backslashes are retained literally (except at the end of a string). This is handy for regular expressions and DOS directory paths; e.g., `r'c:\dir1\file'`.

`u"..."`

> Unicode string constants (see the section "Unicode Strings," later in this book).

Table 7. String constant escape codes

Escape	Meaning	Escape	Meaning
`\newline`	Ignored continuation	`\t`	Horizontal tab
`\\`	Backslash (\)	`\v`	Vertical tab
`\'`	Single quote (')	`\N{id}`	Unicode dbase id
`\"`	Double quote (")	`\uhhhh`	Unicode 16-bit hex
`\a`	Bell	`\Uhhhhhhhh`	Unicode 32-bit hex[a]
`\b`	Backspace	`\xhh`	Hex digits value
`\f`	Formfeed	`\ooo`	Octal digits value
`\n`	Linefeed	`\0`	Null (not end of string)
`\r`	Carriage return	`\other`	Not an escape

[a] `\Uhhhhhhhh` takes exactly eight hexadecimal digits (h); both `\u` and `\U` can be used only in Unicode string constants.

Operations

String operations comprise all sequence operations (shown earlier in Table 3), plus % string formatting expressions, template substitution, and string method calls. Also see the re string pattern-matching module in the section "The re Pattern-Matching Module," and string-related built-in functions in the section "Built-In Functions," both later in this book.

String formatting

String formatting replaces % targets in the string on the left of the % operator, with values on the right (similar to C's sprintf). If more than one value is to be replaced, they must be coded as a tuple to the right of the % operator. If just one item is to be replaced, it can be coded as a single value or one-item tuple on the right. If keynames are used on the left, a dictionary must be supplied on the right.

```
'The knights who say %s!' % 'Ni'
    Result: "The knights who say Ni!"
```

```
"%d %s %d you" % (1, 'spam', 4.0)
    Result: "1 spam 4 you"
```

```
"%(n)d %(x)s" % {"n":1, "x":"spam"}
    Result: "1 spam"
```

%[(*name*)][*flags*][*width*][.*precision*]*code*
    General target format

flags can be - (left-justify), + (numeric sign), a space (leave a blank before positive numbers), and 0 (zero fill); *width* is the total field width; *precision* gives digits after .; and *code* is a character from Table 8. Both *width* and *precision* can be coded as a * to force their values to be taken from the next item in the values to the right of the % operator when sizes are not known until runtime. Hint: %s converts any object to its print representation string.

Table 8. % string formatting codes

Code	Meaning	Code	Meaning
s	String (or any object, uses str( ))	X	x with uppercase
r	s, but uses repr( ), not str( )	e	Floating-point exponent
c	Character	E	e with uppercase
d	Decimal (integer)	f	Floating-point decimal
i	Integer	F	f with uppercase
u	Unsigned (integer)	g	Floating-point e or f
o	Octal integer	G	Floating-point E or F
x	Hex integer	%	Literal '%'

Template string substitution

In Python 2.4, a form of simple string substitution is provided as an alternative to the string formatting described in the prior section. The usual way of substituting variables is with the % operator:

```
>>> '%(page)i: %(title)s' % {'page':2, 'title': 'The Best
of Times'}
'2: The Best of Times'
```

For simpler formatting tasks, a Template class has been added to the string module that uses $ to indicate a substitution:

```
>>> import string
>>> t = string.Template('$page: $title')
>>> t.substitute({'page':2, 'title': 'The Best of Times'})
'2: The Best of Times'
```

Substitution values can be provided as keyword arguments or dictionary keys:

```
>>> s = string.Template('$who likes $what')
>>> s.substitute(who='bob', what=3.14)
'bob likes 3.14'
>>> s.substitute(dict(who='bob', what='pie'))
'bob likes pie'
```

A safe_substitute method ignores missing keys, rather than raising an exception:

```
>>> t = string.SafeTemplate('$page: $title')
>>> t.safe_substitute({'page':3})
'3: $title'
```

String methods

String method calls provide higher-level text processing tools, beyond string expressions. Table 9 lists available string method calls. String methods that modify text always return a new string and never modify the object in-place (strings are immutable). See also the re module in the section "The re Pattern-Matching Module," later in this book, for pattern-based equivalents to many string type methods.

Table 9. String method calls

```
S.capitalize()
S.center(width [, fillchar])
S.count(sub [, start [, end]])
S.decode([encoding [, errors]])
S.encode([encoding [,errors]])
S.endswith(suffix [, start [, end]])
S.expandtabs([tabsize])
S.find(sub [, start [, end]])
S.index(sub [, start [, end]])
S.isalnum()
S.isalpha()
S.isdigit()
S.islower()
S.isspace()
S.istitle()
S.isupper()
S.join(seq)
S.ljust(width [, fillchar])
```

Table 9. String method calls (continued)

```
S.lower()
S.lstrip([chars])
S.replace(old, new [, maxsplit])
S.rfind(sub [,start [,end]])
S.rindex(sub [, start [, end]])
S.rjust(width [, fillchar])
S.rsplit([sep [, maxsplit]])
S.rstrip([chars])
S.split([sep [,maxsplit]])
S.splitlines([keepends])
S.startswith(prefix [, start [, end]])
S.strip([chars])
S.swapcase()
S.title()
S.translate(table [, deletechars])
S.upper()
S.zfill(width)
```

The following sections go into more detail on some of the methods listed in Table 9. In all of the following that return a string result, the result is a new string. (Because strings are immutable, they are never modified in-place.) Whitespace means spaces, tabs, and end-of-line characters (everything in string.whitespace).

Searching

```
s.find(sub, [, start [, end]])
```
> Returns offset of the first occurrence of string sub in s, between offsets start and end (which default to 0 and len(s), the entire string). Returns -1 if not found.

```
s.rfind(sub, [, start [, end]])
```
> Like find, but scans from the end (right to left).

```
s.index(sub [, start [, end]])
```
Like find, but raises ValueError if not found instead of returning -1.

```
s.rindex(sub [, start [, end]])
```
Like rfind, but raises ValueError if not found instead of returning -1.

```
s.count(sub [, start [, end]])
```
Counts the number of nonoverlapping occurrences of sub in s, from offsets start to end (defaults: 0, len(s)).

```
s.startswith(sub [, start [, end]])
```
True if string s starts with substring sub. start and stop give optional begin and end points for matching sub.

```
s.endswith(sub [, start [, end]])
```
True if string s ends with substring sub. start and stop give optional begin and end points for matching sub.

Splitting and joining

```
s.split([sep [, maxsplit]])
```
Returns a list of the words in the string s, using sep as the delimiter string. If maxsplit is given, at most maxsplit splits are done. If sep is not specified or is None, any whitespace string is a separator. 'a*b'.split('*') yields ['a','b']. Use list(s) to convert a string to a list of characters (e.g., ['a','*','b']).

```
sep.join(x)
```
Concatenates a sequence (e.g., list or tuple) of strings x into a single string, with sep added between each item. sep can be '' (an empty string) to convert a list of characters to a string ('*'.join(['a','b']) yields 'a*b').

```
s.replace(old, new [, maxsplit])
```
Returns a copy of string s with all occurrences of substring old replaced by new. If maxsplit is passed, the first maxsplit occurrences are replaced. This works like a combination of x=s.split(old) and new.join(x).

```
s.splitlines([keepends])
```
Splits string s on line breaks, returning lines list. The result does not retain line break characters unless keepends is true.

Formatting

```
s.capitalize()
```
Capitalizes the first character of string s.

```
s.expandtabs([tabsize])
```
Replaces tabs in string s with tabsize spaces (default is 8).

```
s.strip([chars])
```
Removes leading and trailing whitespace from string s (or characters in chars if passed).

```
s.lstrip([chars])
```
Removes leading whitespace from string s (or characters in chars if passed).

```
s.rstrip([chars])
```
Removes trailing whitespace from string s (or characters in chars if passed).

```
s.swapcase()
```
Converts all lowercase letters to uppercase, and vice versa.

```
s.upper()
```
Converts all letters to uppercase.

```
s.lower()
```
Converts all letters to lowercase.

```
s.ljust(width)
```
Left-justifies string s in a field of the given width; pads with spaces on right (can also achieve with % string formatting expression).

`s.rjust(width)`

Right-justifies string s in a field of the given width; pads with spaces on left (can also achieve with % string formatting expression).

`s.center(width)`

Centers string s in a field of the given width; pads with spaces on left and right (can also achieve with % string formatting expression).

`s.zfill(width)`

Pads string s on left with zero digits to produce a string result of the desired width (can also achieve with % string formatting expression).

`s.translate(table [, deletechars])`

Deletes all characters from string s that are in deletechars (if present), then translates the characters using table, a 256-character string giving the translation for each character value indexed by its ordinal.

`s.title()`

Returns a title-cased version of the string: words start with uppercase characters; all remaining cased characters are lowercase.

Content tests

`s.is*()`

The is*() Boolean tests work on strings of any length. They test the content of strings for various categories (and always return False for an empty).

The original string module

Starting in Python 2.0, most of the string-processing functions previously available in the standard string module became available as methods of string objects. If X references a string object, a string module function call such as:

```
import string
res = string.replace(X, 'span', 'spam')
```

is usually equivalent to a string method call such as:

```
res = X.replace('span', 'spam')
```

But the string method call form is preferred and quicker, and string methods require no module imports. Note that the string.join(list, delim) operation becomes a method of the delimiter string delim.join(list).

Unicode Strings

Python supports Unicode (wide) character strings, which represent each character with 16 (or more) bits, not 8.

Literals

Unicode strings are written as u"string". Arbitrary Unicode characters can be written using a special escape sequence, \uHHHH, where HHHH is a four-digit hexadecimal number from 0000 to FFFF. The traditional \xHH escape sequence can also be used, and octal escapes can be used for characters up to +01FF, which is represented by \777.

Operations

Like normal strings, all immutable sequence operations apply. Normal and Unicode string objects can be freely mixed; combining 8-bit and Unicode strings always coerces to Unicode, using the default ASCII encoding (e.g., the result of 'a' + u'bc' is u'abc'). Mixed-type operations assume the 8-bit string contains 7-bit U.S. ASCII data (and raise an error for non-ASCII characters). The built-in str() and unicode() functions can be used to convert between normal and Unicode strings. The encode string method applies a desired encoding scheme to Unicode strings. A handful of related modules (e.g., codecs) and built-in functions are also available. See the Python Library Reference for details.

Lists

Lists are mutable (changeable) arrays of object references, accessed by offset.

Literals and creation

Lists are written as comma-separated series of values enclosed in square brackets.

`[]`
>   An empty list.

`[0, 1, 2, 3]`
>   A four-item list: indexes 0...3.

`alist = ['spam', [42, 3.1415], 1.23, {}]`
>   Nested sublists: alist[1][0] fetches 42.

`alist = list('spam')`
>   Creates a list by calling the type constructor with a sequence.

`alist = [x**2 for x in range(9)]`
>   Creates a list by collecting expression results (list comprehension).

Operations

Operations include all sequence operations (see Table 3, earlier in this book), plus all mutable sequence operations (see Table 4, earlier in this book), plus the following list methods.

`alist.append(x)`
>   Inserts the single object x at the end of alist, changing the list in-place.

`alist.extend(x)`
>   Inserts each item in any sequence x at the end of alist in-place (an in-place +). Similar to alist[len(alist):] = list(x).

```
alist.sort([func [, key [, reverse]]])
```
Sorts alist in-place in ascending order, or per a passed-in two-argument comparison function func (which returns a negative, zero, or positive number to mean the first argument is smaller than, equal to, or larger than the second). key specifies a function of one argument that is used to extract a comparison key from each list element. If reverse is passed and true, the list elements are sorted as if each comparison were reversed.

```
alist.reverse()
```
Reverses items in alist in-place.

```
alist.index(x [, i [, j]])
```
Returns the offset of the first occurrence of object x in alist; raises an exception if not found. This is a search method. If i and j are passed, it returns the smallest k such that s[k] == x and i <= k < j.

```
alist.insert(i, x)
```
Inserts object x into alist at offset i (like alist[i:i] = [x], for positive i).

```
alist.count(x)
```
Returns the number of occurrences of x in alist.

```
alist.remove(x)
```
Deletes the first occurrence of object x from alist; raises an exception if not found.

```
alist.pop([i])
```
Deletes and returns the last (or offset i) item in alist. Use with append to implement stacks. Same as x=alist[i]; del alist[i]; return x, where i defaults to -1, the last item.

List comprehension expressions

A list literal enclosed in square brackets ([...]) can be a simple list of expressions or a list comprehension expression of the following form:

```
[expression for expr1 in sequence1 [if condition]
            for expr2 in sequence2 [if condition] ...
            for exprN in sequenceN [if condition] ]
```

List comprehensions construct result lists: they collect all values of *expression*, for each iteration of all nested for loops, for which each optional *condition* is true. The second through *n*th for loops and all if parts are optional, and *expression* and *condition* can use variables assigned by nested for loops. Names bound inside the comprehension are created in the scope where the comprehension resides.

Comprehensions are similar to the map built-in function:

```
>>> [ord(x) for x in 'spam']
[115, 112, 97, 109]
>>> map(ord, 'spam')
[115, 112, 97, 109]
```

but can often avoid creating a temporary helper function:

```
>>> [x**2 for x in range(5)]
[0, 1, 4, 9, 16]
>>> map((lambda x: x**2), range(5))
[0, 1, 4, 9, 16]
```

Comprehensions with conditions are similar to filter:

```
>>> [x for x in range(5) if x % 2 == 0]
[0, 2, 4]
>>> filter((lambda x: x % 2 == 0), range(5))
[0, 2, 4]
```

Comprehensions with nested for loops are similar to the normal for:

```
>>> [y for x in range(3) for y in range(3)]
[0, 1, 2, 0, 1, 2, 0, 1, 2]

>>> res = []
>>> for x in range(3):
```

```
...         for y in range(3):
...             res.append(y)
>>> res
[0, 1, 2, 0, 1, 2, 0, 1, 2]
```

Generator expressions

In Python 2.4, generator expressions achieve results similar to list comprehensions, without generating a physical list to hold all results. Generator expressions define a set of results, but do not materialize the entire list, to save memory; instead, they create a generator that will return elements one by one in iteration contexts. For example:

```
links = (link for link in get_all_links() if not link.
visited)
for link in links:
    ...
```

Generator expressions are written inside parentheses rather than square brackets. The parentheses used for a function with a single argument suffice when creating an iterator to be passed to a function:

```
print sum(obj.count for obj in list_all_objects())
```

Unlike list comprehensions, generator expression loop variables (obj, in the prior example) are not accessible outside the generator expression. List comprehensions leave the variable assigned to its last value (future versions of Python might change this to make list comprehensions match generator expressions). Use the iterator protocol next method to step through results outside iteration contexts such as for loops, and the list call to produce a list of all results, if required:

```
>>> squares = (x ** 2 for x in range(5))
>>> squares
<generator object at 0x009C7DC8>
>>> squares.next()
0
>>> squares.next()
1
>>> list(x ** 2 for x in range(5))
[0, 1, 4, 9, 16]
```

Dictionaries

Dictionaries are mutable (i.e., changeable) tables of object references, accessed by key, not position. They are unordered collections, implemented internally as dynamically expandable hash tables.

Literals and creation

Dictionaries are written as comma-separated series of *key: value* pairs inside curly braces. Assigning to new keys generates new entries. Any immutable object can be a key (e.g., string, number, tuple), and class instances can be keys if they inherit hashing protocol methods. Tuple keys support compound values (e.g., `adict[(M,D,Y)]`, with parentheses optional).

`{}`
> An empty dictionary.

`{'spam': 2, 'eggs': 3}`
> A two-item dictionary: keys `'spam'` and `'eggs'`.

`adict = { 'info': { 42: 1, type("): 2 }, 'spam': [] }`
> Nested dictionaries: `adict['info'][42]` fetches `1`.

`adict = dict(zip('abc', [1, 2, 3]))`
> Creates a dictionary by passing the key/value tuples list to the type constructor.

`adict = dict(name='Bob', age=42, job=('mgr', 'dev'))`
> Creates a dictionary by passing keyword arguments to the type constructor.

Operations

Operations comprise all mapping operations (see Table 5, earlier in this book), plus the following dictionary-specific methods.

```
adict.has_key(k)
k in adict
```
> Returns True if adict has a key k, or False otherwise.
> Since Python 2.2, k in adict is a generally recom-
> mended alternative to this call (see Table 5).

```
adict.keys()
```
> A new list holding all of adicts keys.[*]

```
adict.values()
```
> A new list holding all the stored values in adict.

```
adict.items()
```
> A new list of tuple pairs (key, value), one for each entry
> in adict.

```
adict.clear()
```
> Removes all items from adict.

```
adict.copy()
```
> Returns a shallow (top-level) copy of adict.

```
dict1.update(dict2)
```
> Merges all of dict2's entries into dict1, in-place, similar to
> for (k, v) in dict2.items(): dict1[k] = v. In Python 2.4,
> also accepts an iterable of key/value pairs, as well as key-
> word arguments (dict.update(k1=v1, k2=v2)).

```
adict.get(key [, default])
```
> Similar to adict[key], but returns default (or None if no
> default) instead of raising an exception when key is not
> found in adict.

```
adict.setdefault(key, [, default])
```
> Same as adict.get(key, default), but also assigns key to
> default if it is not found in adict.

---

[*] As of Python 2.2, dictionary keys can also be iterated over directly. for key
in dict: now has an effect similar to for key in dict.keys(): (and
iterkeys).

```
adict.popitem( )
```
Removes and returns an arbitrary (key, value) pair.

```
adict.pop(k [, x])
```
Returns adict[k] if k in adict (and removes k); else, returns x.

```
adict.fromkeys(seq [, value])
```
Creates a new dictionary with keys from seq and values set to value.

```
adict.iteritems(), adict.iterkeys(), adict.itervalues()
```
Returns an iterator over key/value pairs, keys only, or values only.

Tuples

Tuples are immutable arrays of object references, accessed by offset.

Literals

Tuples are written as comma-separated series of values enclosed in parentheses. The enclosing parentheses can sometimes be omitted (e.g., in for loop headers and = assignments).

```
( )
```
An empty tuple.

```
(0,)
```
A one-item tuple (not a simple expression).

```
(0, 1, 2, 3)
```
A four-item tuple.

```
0, 1, 2, 3
```
Another four-item tuple (same as prior line); not valid in function calls.

```
atuple = ('spam', (42, 'eggs'))
```
Nested tuples: atuple[1][1] fetches 'eggs'.

Operations

All sequence operations (see Table 3, earlier in this book).

Files

The built-in open function creates a *stdio* file object, the most common file interface. File objects export the method calls in the next section. In recent releases, the type name file can be used as a synonym for open when creating a file object (but open is the generally recommended spelling).

Also see the open function in the section "Built-in Functions," later in this book; the anydbm, shelve, and pickle modules in the section "Object Persistence Modules," later in this book; the os module descriptor-based file functions and the os.path directory path tools in the section "The os System Module," later in this book; and the Python SQL database API in the section "Python Portable SQL Database API," later in this book.

Input files

infile = open('data.txt', 'r')
> Creates input file ('r' means read as text, while 'rb' reads binary with no line-break translation). The filename string (e.g., 'data.txt') maps to the current working directory, unless it includes a directory path prefix (e.g., 'c:\\dir\\data.txt'). The mode argument (e.g., 'r') is optional and defaults to 'r'.

infile.read()
> Reads entire file, returning its contents as a single string. In text mode ('r'), line-ends are translated to '\n'. In binary mode ('rb'), the result string can contain nonprintable characters (e.g., '\0').

infile.read(N)
> Reads at most N more bytes (1 or more); empty at end-of-file.

`infile.readline()`
> Reads next line (through end-of-line marker); empty at end-of-file.

`infile.readlines()`
> Reads entire file into a list of line strings. See also file iterators, discussed later in this list.

`infile.xreadlines()`
> Optimized `readlines`. Loads only a few lines at a time into memory, when used in a `for` loop header. Deprecated since Version 2.3. Use file iterators instead (discussed next).

`for line in infile:`
> Uses file iterators to step through lines in a file. Also available in other iteration contexts (e.g., `[line[:-1] for line in open('filename')]`). As of Python 2.2, files can be iterated over directly. `for line in fileobj:` has an effect similar to `for line in fileobj.readlines():`, but the file iterator is more efficient.

Output files

`outfile = open('/tmp/spam', 'w')`
> Creates output file. (Note that `'w'` means write text; `'wb'` writes binary data with no line-break translation).

`outfile.write(S)`
> Writes string S onto file (all bytes in S, with no formatting applied). In text mode, `'\n'` is translated to the platform-specific line-end marker sequence. In binary mode, the string can contain nonprintable bytes (e.g., use `'a\0b\0c'` to write a string of five bytes, two of which are binary zero).

`outfile.writelines(L)`
> Writes all strings in list L onto file.

Any files

`file.close()`
> Manual close to free resources (Python currently auto-closes files when they are garbage-collected).

`file.tell()`
> Returns the file's current position (like C's `ftell`).

`file.seek(offset [, whence])`
> Sets the current file position to `offset` for random access (like C's `fseek`). `whence` can be 0 (offset from front), 1 (offset +/- from current position), or 2 (offset from end). `whence` defaults to 0.

`file.isatty()`
> Returns `1` if the file is connected to a tty-like interactive device.

`file.flush()`
> Flushes the file's `stdio` buffer (like C's `fflush`). Useful for buffered pipes, if another process (or human) is reading. Also useful for files created and read in the same process.

`file.truncate([size])`
> Truncates file to, at most, `size` bytes (or current position if no size is passed). Not available on all platforms.

`file.fileno()`
> Gets file number (descriptor integer) for file. This roughly converts file objects to descriptors that can be passed to tools in the `os` module. Use `os.fdopen` to convert a descriptor to a file object, `socketobj.makefile` to convert a socket to a file object, and `StringIO.StringIO` to convert a string to an object with a file-like interface.

Attributes (all read-only)

`file.closed`
> True if file has been closed

`file.mode`
> Mode string (e.g., `'r'`) passed to open function

`file.name`
> String name of corresponding external file

Notes

- Some file-open modes (e.g., `'r+'`) allow a file to be both input and output, and others (e.g., `'rb'`) specify binary-mode transfer to suppress line-end marker conversions. See open in the section "Built-in Functions," later in this book.

- File-transfer operations occur at the current file position, but seek method calls reposition the file for random access.

- File transfers can be made *unbuffered*: see open in the section "Built-in Functions," later in this book, and the -u command-line flag in the section "Command-Line Options," earlier in this book.

Other Common Types

As of Python 2.4, explicit Booleans, sets, and a numeric decimal type are also available.

Boolean

The Boolean type, named `bool`, provides two predefined constants, named `True` and `False` (available since Version 2.3). For most purposes, these constants can be treated as though they were pre-assigned to integers 1 and 0, respectively (e.g., `True + 3` yields 4). However, the bool type is a subclass of the integer type, `int`, and customizes it to print instances differently (True prints as "True", not "1").

Sets

Set objects are generated with the built-in functions set(*iterable*) and frozenset(*iterable*) (frozen sets are immutable, and similar types were available in a module in Version 2.3). Sets provide common set operations such as membership, intersection, and union:

```
>>> x = set('abcde')
>>> y = set('bdxyz')
>>> x
set(['a', 'c', 'b', 'e', 'd'])
>>> 'e' in x                          # membership
True
>>> x - y                            # difference
set(['a', 'c', 'e'])
>>> x | y                            # union
set(['a', 'c', 'b', 'e', 'd', 'y', 'x', 'z'])
>>> x & y                            # intersection
set(['b', 'd'])
```

Decimal

As of Python 2.4, a numeric type is available in the decimal module, for applications where the potential inaccuracies of floating-point hardware are significant (e.g., for representing money). For instance, normal floating-point objects cannot exactly represent some values:

```
>>> 35.72 + 1.73
37.449999999999996
>>> 35.72 - 1.73
33.990000000000002
```

Decimal objects retain correct results:

```
>>> import decimal
>>> a = decimal.Decimal('35.72')
>>> b = decimal.Decimal('1.73')
>>> a + b
Decimal("37.45")
>>> a - b
Decimal("33.99")
```

A Context object in this module allows for specifying precision (number of decimal digits) and rounding modes (down, ceiling, etc.):

```
>>> decimal.Decimal(1) / decimal.Decimal(7)
Decimal("0.1428571428571428571428571429")
>>> decimal.getcontext().prec = 4
>>> decimal.Decimal(1) / decimal.Decimal(7)
Decimal("0.1429")
```

Type Conversions

Tables 10 and 11 define common built-in tools for converting from one type to another.

Table 10. Sequence converters

Converter	Converts from	Converts to
list(X) map(None, X) [n for n in X][a]	String, tuple, user-defined sequence, any iterable	List
tuple(X)	String, list, user-defined sequence, any iterable	Tuple
''.join(X)	Sequence of strings	String

[a] The list comprehension form is much slower than list(), and list() has made this form of map(None, ...) obsolete since Version 2.2.

Table 11. String/object converters

Converter	Converts from	Converts to
eval(S)	String	Any object with a syntax (expression)
int(S [, base])[a] float(S) long(S [, base])	String or number	Integer, float, long
repr(X) str(X) `X` (back quotes)	Any Python object	String (repr is as code, str is user-friendly, back quotes yield the same as repr)
X % Y (string formatting)	Objects with format codes	String

Table 11. String/object converters (continued)

Converter	Converts from	Converts to
hex(X), oct(X), str(X)	Integer types	Hexadecimal, octal, decimal strings
ord(C), chr(I)	Character, integer code	Integer code, character

[a] In Version 2.2, converter functions (e.g., int, float, str) are also available as class constructors, and can be subclassed.

Statements and Syntax

This section describes the rules for syntax and variable names.

Syntax Rules

Here are the general rules for writing Python programs.

Control flow
> Statements execute one after another, unless control-flow statements are used (if, while, for, raise, calls, etc.).

Blocks
> A block is delimited by indenting all of its statements by the same amount, with spaces or tabs. A tab counts for enough spaces to move the column to a multiple of 8. Blocks can appear on the same line as a statement header if they are simple statements.

Statements
> A statement ends at the end of a line, but can continue over multiple lines if a physical line ends with a \, an unclosed ( ), [], or {} pair, or an unclosed, triple-quoted string. Multiple simple statements can appear on a line if they are separated with a semicolon (;).

Comments
> Comments start with a # (not in a string constant) and span to the end of the line.

Documentation strings
> If a function, module file, or class begins with a string literal, it is stored in the object's __doc__ attribute. See the help( ) function, and the pydoc module and script in the Python Library Reference for automated extraction and display tools.

Whitespace
> Generally significant only to the left of code, where indentation is used to group blocks. Blank lines and spaces are otherwise ignored except as token separators and within string constants.

Name Rules

This section contains the rules for user-defined names (i.e., variables) in programs.

Name format

Structure
> User-defined names start with a letter or underscore (_), followed by any number of letters, digits, or underscores.

Reserved words
> User-defined names cannot be the same as any Python reserved word listed in Table 12.[*]

Case sensitivity
> User-defined names and reserved words are always case-sensitive: *SPAM*, *spam*, and *Spam* are different names.

Unused tokens
> Python does not use the characters $ and ? in its syntax, though they can appear in string constants and comments, and $ is special in string template substitution.

---

[*] In the Jython Java-based implementation, user-defined names can sometimes be the same as reserved words.

Creation

User-defined names are created by assignment but must exist when referenced (e.g., counters must be explicitly initialized to zero). See the section "Namespace and Scope Rules," later in this book.

Table 12. Reserved words

and	assert	break	class	continue
def	del	elif	else	except
exec	finally	for	from	global
if	import	in	is	lambda
not	or	pass	print	raise
return	try	while	yield	

Name conventions

- Names that begin and end with two underscores (for example, __init__) have a special meaning to the interpreter but are not reserved words.

- Names beginning with one underscore (e.g., _X) and assigned at the top level of a module are not copied out by from...* imports (see also the __all__ module export names list, mentioned in the sections "The from Statement" and "Pseudo-Private Attributes," later in this book).

- Names beginning but not ending with two underscores (e.g., __X) within a class statement are prefixed with the enclosing class's name (see the section "Pseudo-Private Attributes," later in this book).

- The name that is just a single underscore (_) is used in the interactive interpreter (only) to store the result of the last evaluation.

- Built-in function and exception names (e.g., open, SyntaxError) are not reserved words. They live in the last-searched scope and can be reassigned to hide the built-in meaning in the current scope (e.g., open=42).

- Class names commonly begin with an uppercase letter (e.g., MyClass).
- The first (leftmost) argument in a class method function is commonly named self.

Specific Statements

The following sections describe all Python statements. Each section lists the statement's syntax formats, followed by usage details. For compound statements, each appearance of a *suite* in a statement format stands for one or more other statements, possibly indented as a block under a header line. A suite must be indented under a header if it contains another compound statement (if, while, etc.); otherwise, it can appear on the same line as the statement header. The following are both valid constructs:

```
if x < 42:
    print x
    while x: x = x -1

if x < 42: print x
```

Assignment

```
target = expression
target1 = target2 = expression
target1, target2 = expression1, expression2
target1, target2,... = same-length-sequence
(target1, target2,...) = same-length-sequence
[target1, target2,...] = same-length-sequence
```

Assignments store references to objects in targets. Expressions yield objects. Targets can be simple names (X), qualified attributes (X.attr), or indexes and slices (X[i], X[i:j]).

The second format assigns an *expression* object to each target. The third format pairs targets with expressions, left to right. The last three formats assign components of any sequence to corresponding targets, from left to right. The sequence on the right must be the same length, but can be any type.

Augmented assignment

A set of additional assignment statement formats, listed in Table 13, are available. Known as *augmented assignments*, these formats imply a binary expression plus an assignment. For instance, the following two formats are roughly equivalent:

```
X = X + Y
X += Y
```

However, the reference to target X in the second format needs to be evaluated only once, and in-place operations can be applied for mutables as an optimization (e.g., list1 += list2 automatically calls list1.extend(list2), instead of the slower concatenation operation implied by +). Classes can overload in-place assignments with method names that begin with an i (e.g., __iadd__ for +=, __add__ for +). The format X //= Y (floor division) is new as of Version 2.2.

Table 13. Augmented assignment statements

X += Y	X &= Y	X -= Y	X |= Y
X *= Y	X ^= Y	X /= Y	X >>= Y
X %= Y	X <<= Y	X **= Y	X //= Y

Expressions

```
expression
function([value, name=value, ...])
object.method([value, name=value, ...])
```

Any expression can appear as a statement (but statements cannot appear as expressions). Expressions are commonly used for calling functions and for interactive-mode printing.

In function and method calls, actual arguments are separated by commas and are normally matched to arguments in function def headers by position. Calls can optionally list specific argument names in functions to receive passed values by using the *name=value* keyword syntax.

apply( )-like call syntax

As of Python 2.0, special syntax can be used in function and method call argument lists to achieve the same effect as an apply() built-in function call. If *args* and *kw* are a tuple and a dictionary, respectively, the following are equivalent:

```
apply(f, args, kw)
f(*args, **kw)
```

Both formats call function f with a positional arguments sequence of *args* and a keyword arguments dictionary of *kw*. The latter format is intended to be symmetric with function header arbitrary-argument syntax such as def f(*args, **kw):. It is also more flexible, since it can be more easily combined with positional and keyword arguments (e.g., f(1,2,foo=3,bar=4,*args,**kw)).

The print Statement

```
print [value [, value]* [,]]
print >> fileobj [, value [,value]* [,]]
```

print displays the printable representation of values on a stdout stream (the current setting of sys.stdout) as well as adds spaces between values. The trailing comma suppresses the linefeed that is normally added at the end of a list. Because print simply calls the write method of the object currently referenced by sys.stdout, the following is equivalent to print X:

```
import sys
sys.stdout.write(str(X) + '\n')
```

To redirect print text to files or class objects, reassign sys.stdout to any object with a write method:

```
sys.stdout = open('log', 'a')  # any object with a write()
print "Warning-bad spam!"  # goes to the object's write()
```

Extended print form

The print statement can also name an open output file-like object to be the target of the printed text (instead of sys. stdout):

```
fileobj = open('log', 'a')
print >> fileobj, "Warning-bad spam!"
```

If the file object is None, sys.stdout is used. Because sys. stdout can be reassigned, the >> form is not strictly needed; however, it can often avoid both explicit write method calls and saving and restoring the original sys.stdout value around a redirected print.

The if Statement

```
if test:
    suite
[elif test:
    suite]*
[else:
    suite]
```

The if statement selects from among one or more actions (statement blocks), and it runs the suite associated with the first if or elif test that is true, or the else suite if all are false.

The while Statement

```
while test:
    suite
[else:
    suite]
```

The while loop is a general loop that keeps running the first suite while the test at the top is true. It runs the else suite if the loop exits without hitting a break statement.

The for Statement

```
for target in sequence:
    suite
[else:
    suite]
```

The for loop is a sequence iteration that assigns items in *sequence* to *target* and runs the first suite for each. The for statement runs the else suite if the loop exits without hitting a break statement. *target* can be anything that can appear on the left side of an = assignment statement (e.g., for (x, y) in tuplelist:).

In Version 2.2, this works by first trying to obtain an *iterator* object with iter(sequence) and then calling that object's next() method repeatedly until StopIteration is raised (see the section "The yield Statement," later in this book). In earlier versions, or if no iterator object can be obtained (e.g., no __iter__ method is defined), this works instead by repeatedly indexing *sequence* at successively higher offsets until an IndexError is raised.

The pass Statement

```
pass
```

This is a do-nothing placeholder statement, and is used when syntactically necessary.

The break Statement

```
break
```

This immediately exits the closest enclosing while or for loop statement, skipping its associated else (if any).

The continue Statement

```
continue
```

This immediately goes to the top of the closest enclosing while or for loop statement; it resumes in the loop header line.

The del Statement

```
del name
del name[i]
del name[i:j]
del name.attribute
```

The del statement deletes names, items, slices, and attributes, as well as removes bindings. In the last three forms, *name* can actually be any expression (with parentheses if required for priority). For instance: del a.b()[1].c.d.

The exec Statement

```
exec codestring [in globaldict [, localdict]]
```

The exec statement compiles and runs code strings. *codestring* is any Python statement (or multiple statements separated by newlines) as a string; it is run in a namespace containing the exec, or the global/local namespace dictionaries if specified (*localdict* defaults to *globaldict*). *codestring* can also be a compiled code object. The backward-compatible syntax exec(a, b, c) is also accepted. Also see compile, eval, and execfile in the section "Built-in Functions," later in this book.

The def Statement

```
def name([arg,... arg=value,... *arg, **arg]):
    suite
```

The def statement makes new functions. It creates a function object and assigns it to variable *name*. Each call to a function object generates a new, local scope, where assigned

---

names are local to the function call by default (unless declared global). See also the section "Namespace and Scope Rules," later in this book. Arguments are passed by assignment; in a def header, they can be defined by any of the four formats in Table 14.

Table 14. Argument formats in definitions

Argument format	Interpretation
arg	Matched by name or position
arg=value	Default value if arg is not passed
*arg	Collects extra positional args as a new tuple
**arg	Collects extra keyword args passed as a new dictionary

All four forms in Table 14 can also be used in a function call, where they are interpreted as shown in Table 15.

Table 15. Argument formats in calls

Argument format	Interpretation
arg	Positional argument
arg=value	Keyword (match by name) argument
*arg	Sequence of positional arguments
**arg	Dictionary of keyword arguments

Mutable default argument values are evaluated once at def statement time, not on each call, and so can retain state between calls (however, classes are better state-retention tools, and this behavior is often considered a caveat):

```
>>> def grow(a, b=[]):
...     b.append(a)
...     print b
...
>>> grow(1); grow(2)
[1]
[1, 2]
```

lambda expressions

Functions can also be created with the lambda expression form:

```
lambda arg, arg,...: expression
```

In lambda, *arg* is as in def, *expression* is the implied return value, and the generated function is simply returned as the lambda result to be called later, instead of being assigned to a variable. Because lambda is an expression, not a statement, it can be used in places that a def cannot (e.g., within a dictionary literal expression, or an argument list of a function call).

Function and method decorators

As of Python 2.4, function definitions can be preceded by a declaration syntax that describes the function which follows. Known as *decorators* and coded with an @ character, these declarations replace previous functional techniques. For example, the original way to define a static method:

```
class C:
    def meth():
        ...
    meth = staticmethod(meth)    # Rebind name
```

can be coded with decorator syntax:

```
class C:
    @staticmethod
    def meth():
        ...
```

The decorator version works identically to the original form because an @declaration preceding a definition of a function F is roughly shorthand for an F=declaration(F) assignment following the definition. More generally, the following:

```
@A
@B
@C
def f(): ...
```

is roughly equivalent to the following nondecorator code:

```
def f(): ...
f = A(B(C(f)))
```

Decorators must appear on the line before a function definition, and cannot be on the same line (meaning @A def f(): ... is illegal). Decorators can only be applied to function definitions, either at the module level or inside a class; they cannot be applied to class definitions. Decorators also take argument lists:

```
@foo(1,2,3)
def f(): ...
```

In this case foo must be a function returning a function (known as a *metafunction*).

The return Statement

```
return [expression]
```

The return statement exits the enclosing function and returns an *expression* value as the result of the call to the function. The *expression* defaults to None if it's omitted. Hint: return a tuple for multiple-value function results.

The yield Statement

```
yield expression
```

The yield statement suspends function state and returns an *expression*. On the next iteration, the function's prior state is restored, and control resumes immediately after the yield statement. Use a return statement with no value to end the iteration, or simply fall off the end of the function:

```
def generate_ints(N):
    for i in xrange(N):
        yield i
```

The yeild statement is standard as of Version 2.3 and later; in Version 2.2, enable it with from __future__ import generators.

Generators and iterators

Functions containing a `yield` statement are compiled as *generators*; when called, they return a generator object that supports the iterator interface (i.e., a `next()` method).

Iterators are objects returned by the `iter(X)` built-in function; they define a `next()` method, which returns the next item in the iteration or raises a `StopIteration` exception to end the iteration.

Iteration contexts automatically use the iteration protocol to step through collections. Classes can provide an `__iter__` method to overload the `iter(X)` built-in function call; if defined, the result is used to step through objects in `for` loops, rather than the traditional `__getitem__` indexing overload scheme.

The global Statement

```
global name [, name]*
```

The `global` statement is a namespace declaration: when used inside a class or function, it treats appearances of *name* as references to a global (module-level) variable by that name—whether it is assigned or not. Because of Python scope rules, you need to declare only global names that are assigned within a `def` (global references are automatically found in the enclosing module).

The import Statement

```
import module [, module]*
import [package.]* module [, [package.]* module]*
import [package.]* module as name [, [package.]*module as
name]*
```

The `import` statement provides module access: it imports a module as a whole. Modules contain names fetched by qualification (e.g., *module.attribute*). module names the target module—a Python file or compiled module located in a directory in sys.path (e.g., PYTHONPATH), without its filename suffix (.*py* and other extensions are omitted). Assignments at the top level of a Python file create module object attributes. The as clause assigns a variable *name* to the imported module object; it is useful to provide shorter synonyms for long module names.

Import operations compile a file's source to byte-code if needed (and save it in a .*pyc* file if possible), then execute the compiled code from top to bottom to generate module object attributes by assignment. Use the reload built-in function to force recompilation and execution of already-loaded modules; see also __import__ used by import, in the section "Built-in Functions," later in this book.

In the Jython implementation, imports can also name Java class libraries; Jython generates a Python module wrapper that interfaces with the Java library. In standard (C) Python, imports can also load compiled C and C++ extensions.

Package imports

If used, the *package* prefix names give enclosing directory names, and module dotted paths reflect directory hierarchies. An import of the form import dir1.dir2.mod generally loads the module file at directory path *dir1/dir2/mod.py*, where *dir1* must be contained by a directory listed on the module search python (e.g., PYTHONPATH, .*pth* files, or the program's home directory). Each directory listed in an import statement must have a (possibly empty) __init__.py file that serves as the directory level's module namespace. This file is run on the first import through the directory, and all names assigned in __init__.py files become attributes of the directory's module object. Directory packages can resolve conflicts caused by the linear nature of PYTHONPATH.

The from Statement

```
from [package.]* module import name [,name]*
from [package.]* module import *
from [package.]* module import name as othername
from [package.]* module import (name1, name2,
                                name3, name4)
```

The from statement imports variable names from a module so that you can use those names later without the need to qualify them with their module name. The from mod import * format copies *all* names assigned at the top level of the module, except names with a single leading underscore or names not listed in the module's __all__ list-of-strings attribute (if defined).

If used, the as clause creates a name synonym. If used, *package* import paths work the same as in import statements (e.g., from dir1.dir2.mod import X), but the package path needs to be listed only in the from itself. Due to new scoping rules, the * format generates warnings in Version 2.2 if it appears nested in a function or class.

As of Python 2.4, the names being imported from a module can be enclosed in parentheses to span multiple lines without backslashes.

The from statement is also used to enable future (but still experimental) language additions, with from __future__ import *featurename*. This format must appear only at the top of a module file (preceded only by an optional doc string).

The class Statement

```
class name [ ( super [, super]* ) ]:
    suite
```

The class statement makes new class objects, which are factories for instance objects. Also, it builds a new class object and assigns it to variable *name*. The class statement introduces a new local name scope, and all names assigned in the class statement generate class object attributes shared by all instances of the class. Important class features include the following (see also the sections "Object-Oriented Programming" and "Operator Overloading Methods," later in this book):

- Superclasses (also known as base classes) from which a new class inherits attributes are listed in parentheses in the header (e.g., class Sub(Super1, Super2):).

- Assignments in the suite generate class attributes inherited by instances: nested def statements make methods, while assignment statements make simple class members, etc.

- Calling the class generates instance objects. Each instance object has its own attributes and inherits the attributes of the class and all of its superclasses.

- Specially named method definitions overload operations.

The try Statement

```
try:
    suite
[except [name [, data]]:
    suite]*
[else:
    suite]

try:
    suite
finally:
    suite
```

The try statement catches exceptions. try statements can specify except clauses with suites that serve as handlers for exceptions raised during the try suite, else clauses that run if no exception occurs during the try suite, and finally clauses that run whether an exception happens or not.

Exceptions can be raised by Python, or explicitly (see also the raise statement discussed in the next section, "The raise Statement"). In except clauses, an extra variable name (*data*)

---

can be used to intercept an extra data item raised with the
exception name, or the class instance raised. Table 16 lists all
the clauses that can appear in a try statement. finally cannot be mixed with except or else, and try/finally interacts
correctly with return, break, and continue (if any of these
pass control out of the try block, the finally clause is executed on the way out).

Table 16. Try statement clause formats

Clause format	Interpretation
except:	Catch all (other) exceptions.
except name:	Catch a specific exception only.
except name, value:	Catch exception and extra data.
except (name1, name2):	Catch any of the exceptions.
else:	Run if no exceptions are raised.
finally:	Always run on the way out.

Common variations include the following.

except *classname*, X:
> Catch a class exception, and assign X to the raised
> instance.

except (*name1*, *name2*, *name2*), X:
> Catch any of the exceptions, and assign X to the extra
> data.

The raise Statement

raise *string*
> Matches an except handler clause that names the raised
> string object.

raise *string*, *data*
> Passes an extra *data* object with an exception (the default
> is None); it is assigned to variable X in an except string,
> X: try statement clause.

raise *instance*

> This is the same as raise instance.__class__, instance.

raise *class, instance*

> Matches an except that names this *class*, or any of its superclasses. Passes the class *instance* object as extra data with an exception, to be assigned to *X* in an except *class, X*: try statement clause.

raise

> Re-raises the current exception.

The raise statement triggers exceptions. Control jumps to the matching except clause of the most recently entered matching try statement, or to the top level of the process (where it ends the program and prints a standard error message). You can use this to raise built-in or user-defined exceptions. Without arguments, raise re-raises the most recent exception. See also the section "Built-in Exceptions," later in this book, for exceptions raised by Python.

Class exceptions

Exceptions can be string objects (first two formats) or class instances (second two formats). try statement except clauses that name string objects are matched by string identity (is), not by value (==). try statement except clauses that name classes catch an instance of that class, as well as any of its subclasses. All built-in exceptions are now class objects.

Class exceptions support exception *categories*, which can be easily extended. Because try statements catch all subclasses when they name a superclass, exception categories can be modified by altering the set of subclasses without breaking existing try statements. The raised instance object also provides storage for extra information about the exception:

```
class General:
    def __init__(self, x):
        self.data = x
class Specific1(General): pass
```

```
class Specific2(General): pass

try:
    raise Specific1('spam')
except General, X:
    print X.data                # prints 'spam'
```

For backward compatibility with prior Python releases that supported only string exceptions, these raise formats are also allowed:

```
raise class [, arg]
raise class, (arg, arg,...)
```

These formats are the same as the instance format raise *class*([*arg*...]). The first format occurs when *arg* is not an instance of *class*. Python generates and raises an instance automatically, even if the raise lists only a class name (i.e., raise *Class* is the same as raise *Class( )*). It is suggested but not required that user-defined exceptions inherit from the built-in exception class Exception (see the section "Built-in Exceptions," later in this book).

The assert Statement

```
assert expression [, message]
```

The assert statement performs debugging checks. If *expression* is false, it raises AssertionError, passing *message* as an extra data item if specified. The -0 command-line flag removes assertion logic.

Namespace and Scope Rules

This section discusses rules for name binding and lookup (see also the sections "Name format" and "Name conventions," earlier in this book). In all cases, names are created when first assigned but must already exist when referenced. Qualified and unqualified names are resolved differently.

Qualified Names: Object Namespaces

Qualified names (X, in object.X) are known as *attributes* and live in object namespaces. Assignments in some lexical scopes[*] initialize object namespaces (modules, classes).

Assignment: object.X = value
> Creates or alters the attribute name X in the namespace of the object being qualified.

Reference: object.X
> Searches for the attribute name X in the object, then all accessible classes above it (for instances and classes). This is the definition of *inheritance*.

Unqualified Names: Lexical Scopes

Unqualified names (X) involve lexical scope rules. Assignments bind such names to the local scope, unless they are declared global.

Assignment: X = value
> Makes name X local: creates or changes name X in the current local scope by default. If X is declared global, this creates or changes name X in the enclosing module's scope. Local variables are stored in the call stack for quick access.

Reference: X
> Prior to Version 2.2, looks for name X in at most three scopes: the current *local* scope (function), then the current *global* scope (module), then the *built-in* scope (module __builtin__). Local and global scope contexts are defined in Table 17.
>
> In Version 2.2 and later, this looks for name X in the current local scope (function), then in the local scopes of all lexically enclosing functions (if any, from inner to outer),

---

[*] Lexical scopes refer to physically nested code structures in a program's source code.

then in the current global scope (module), then in the built-in scope (module `__builtin__`). Global declarations make the search begin in the global scope instead.

Table 17. Unqualified name scopes

Code context	Global scope	Local scope
Module	Same as local	The module itself
Function, method	Enclosing module	Function call
Class	Enclosing module	`class` statement
Script, interactive mode	Same as local	`module __main__`
`exec, eval`	Caller's global (or passed in)	Caller's local (or passed in)

Statically Nested Scopes

The enclosing scope search of the last rule in the previous section (Reference: X) is called a *statically nested scope*, and was made standard in Version 2.2. For example, the following function works as is in Version 2.2 and later because the reference to x within f2 has access to the scope of f1:

```
def f1():
    x = 42
    def f2():
        print x
    f2()
```

In Python versions prior to 2.2 this function fails because name x is not local (in f2's scope), global (in the module enclosing f1), or built-in. To make such cases work prior to Version 2.2, default arguments are typically used to retain values from the immediately enclosing scope (defaults are evaluated before entering a def):

```
def f1():
    x = 42
    def f2(x=x):
        print x
    f2()
```

This rule also applies to lambda expressions, which imply a nested scope just like def and are more commonly nested in practice:

```
def func():
    x = 42
    action = (lambda n: x ** n)          # works in 2.2

def func():
    x = 42
    action = (lambda n, x=x: x ** n)     # use before 2.2
```

Scopes nest arbitrarily, but only enclosing functions (not classes) are searched:

```
def f1():
    x = 42
    def f2():
        def f3():
            print x      # found in f1's scope
        f3()
    f2()
```

As a consequence of this change in Version 2.2, the following constructs are no longer valid within a function body: from module import *, and exec statements without explicit namespace dictionaries. Both constructs can assign unknown names and so prevent the compiler from detecting names defined in enclosing scopes. Programs can also fail as of Version 2.2 if they use the same name in both the global and a lexically enclosing function's scope; the enclosing function's name now hides the global.

Object-Oriented Programming

Classes are Python's main object-oriented programming (OOP) tool. They support multiple instances, attribute inheritance, and operator overloading.

Classes and Instances

Class objects provide default behavior

- The class statement creates a *class* object and assigns it to a name.
- Assignments inside class statements create class *attributes*, which export object state and behavior.
- Class *methods* are nested defs, with special first arguments to receive the instance.

Instance objects are generated from classes

- Calling a class object like a function makes a new *instance* object.
- Each instance object inherits class attributes and gets its own attribute *namespace*.
- Assignments to attributes of the first argument (e.g., self.X = V) in methods create per-instance *attributes*.

Inheritance rules

- Inheritance happens at attribute qualification time: on object.attribute, if object is a class or instance.
- Classes inherit attributes from all classes listed in their class statement header line (superclasses). Listing more than one means *multiple inheritance*.
- Instances inherit attributes from the class from which they are generated, plus all that class's superclasses.
- Inheritance searches the instance, then its class, then all accessible superclasses (depth-first, and left-to-right), and uses the first version of an attribute name found.

Pseudo-Private Attributes

By default, all attribute names in modules and classes are visible everywhere. Special conventions allow some limited data-hiding, but are mostly designed to prevent name collisions (see also the section "Name conventions," earlier in this book).

Module privates

Names in modules with a single underscore (e.g., _X), and those not listed on the module's __all__ list, are not copied over when a client uses from module import *. This is not strict privacy, though, as such names can still be accessed apart from the from..* statement.

Class privates

Names anywhere within class statements with two leading underscores only (e.g., __X) are mangled at compile time to include the enclosing class name as a prefix (e.g., _Class__X). The added class-name prefix localizes such names to the enclosing class and thus makes them distinct in both the self instance object and the class hierarchy.

This helps to avoid clashes that arise in the single instance object at the bottom of the inheritance chain (all assignments to self.attr anywhere in a framework change the single instance namespace). This is not strict privacy, though, as such attributes can still be accessed via the mangled name.

New Style Classes

In Version 2.2 and later, inheritance search order can be slightly different in multiple inheritance diamonds if a superclass inherits from object (e.g., class A(object)) but is still strictly depth-first and then left-to-right otherwise. In new style classes, superclasses are searched across before climbing the class tree. New style classes also introduce a handful of new class features.

Operator Overloading Methods

Classes intercept and implement built-in operations by providing specially named method functions, all of which start and end with two underscores. These names are not reserved and can be inherited from superclasses as usual. At most, one is located and called per operation.

Python automatically calls a class's overloading methods when instances appear in expressions and other contexts. For example, if a class defines a method named __getitem__, and X is an instance of this class, the expression X[i] is equivalent to the method call X.__getitem__(i).

Overloading method names are sometimes arbitrary: a class's __add__ method need not perform an addition (or concatenation). Moreover, classes generally can mix numeric and collection methods and mutable and nonmutable operations.

For All Types

__init__(self [, arg]*)
> Invoked on class(args...). This is a constructor that initializes the new instance, self.

__del__(self)
> Invoked on instance garbage collection. This method cleans up when an instance is freed. Embedded objects are automatically freed when the parent is (unless referenced from elsewhere).

__repr__(self)
> Invoked on `self`, repr(self) and print self (if there is no __str__). This method returns a string representation.

__str__(self)
> Invoked on str(self) and print self (or uses __repr__ if defined). This method returns a string representation.

`__cmp__(self, other)`, `__rcmp__`

Invoked on self > x, x == self, cmp(self, x), etc. This method is called for all comparisons for which no more specific method (such as `__lt__`) is defined or inherited. It returns -1, 0, or 1 for self less than, equal to, or greater than other. If no rich comparison or `__cmp__` methods are defined, class instances compare by their identity (address in memory). Note: the `__rcmp__` right-side method is no longer supported as of Version 2.1.

`__hash__(self)`

Invoked on dictionary[self] and hash(self). This method returns a unique and unchanging integer hash-key.

`__call__(self [, arg]*)`

Invoked on self(args...), when an instance is called like a function.

`__getattr__(self, name)`

Invoked on self.name, when name is an undefined attribute access (this method is not called if name exists in or is inherited by self). name is a string. This method returns an object or raises AttributeError.

`__setattr__(self, name, value)`

Invoked on self.name=value (all attribute assignments). Hint: assign through `__dict__` key to avoid loops: self.attr=x statement within a `__setattr__` calls `__setattr__` again, but self.`__dict__`['attr']=x does not.

`__delattr__(self, name)`

Invoked on del self.name (all attribute deletions).

`__getattribute__(self, name)`

Called unconditionally to implement attribute accesses for instances of the class. If the class also defines `__getattr__`, it will never be called (unless it is called explicitly). This method should return the (computed) attribute value or raise an AttributeError exception. To avoid infinite recursion in this method, its implementation should always call the base class method with the same name to access any attributes it needs (e.g., `object.__getattribute__(self, name)`).

`__lt__(self, other)`
`__le__(self, other)`
`__eq__(self, other)`
`__ne__(self, other)`
`__gt__(self, other)`
`__ge__(self, other)`

Respectively, used on self < other, self <= other, self == other, self != other, and self <> other, self > other, self >= other. Added in Version 2.1, these are knows as *rich comparison* methods and are called for comparison operators in preference to `__cmp__` (as discussed earlier). For example, X < Y calls X.`__lt__`(Y) if defined; otherwise, it tries X.`__cmp__`(Y).

These methods can return any value, but if the comparison operator is used in a Boolean context, the return value is interpreted as a Boolean result for the operator. These methods can also return the special object `NotImplemented`, which forces Python to revert to the general `__cmp__` method.

There are no right-side (swapped-argument) versions of these methods to be used when the left argument does not support the operation but the right argument does. `__lt__` and `__gt__` are each other's reflection, `__le__` and `__ge__` are each other's reflection, and `__eq__` and `__ne__` are their own reflections.

`__slots__`

This class variable can be assigned a string, iterable, or sequence of strings with variable names used by instances. If defined in a new-style class, `__slots__` reserves space for the declared variables and prevents the automatic creation of `__dict__` for each instance.

For Collections (Sequences, Mappings)

__len__(self)
>   Invoked on len(self) for truth-value tests. This method returns a sequence or mapping collection size. Zero length means false. For Boolean tests, it looks for __ nonzero__ first, then __len__, and then is considered true.

__contains__(self, item)
>   Invoked on item in self for sequence membership tests (otherwise, it uses __iter__, if defined, or __getitem__). This method returns 1 or 0 for true or false.

__iter__(self)
>   Invoked on iter(self). New in Version 2.2, this method is a sequence iteration generator. It returns an object with a next() method (possibly self). The result object's next() method is called repeatedly in all iteration contexts (e.g., for loops). This method should raise StopIteration to terminate the progression (see also the section "The yield Statement," earlier in this book).

As of Python 2.0, the following three methods can also be called for slice operations. For sequence types, the accepted keys should be integers and slice objects. Slice objects have the attributes start, stop, and step, any of which can be None. See also the slice methods later in this section.

__getitem__(self, key)
>   Invoked on self[key], x in self, and for x in self. This method implements all indexing-related operations. Membership and iteration (in and for) repeatedly index from 0 until IndexError, unless __iter__ is defined. In Version 2.0, it can also be passed a slice object for some slice operations.

__setitem__(self, key, value)
>   Invoked on self[key]=value. This method is the assignment to a collection key or index.

```
__delitem__(self, key)
```
> Invoked on del self[key]. This method is for index/key component deletion.

As of Python 2.0, the following three methods are considered deprecated, but are still supported. They are called only when a simple two-item slice with a single colon is used and the slice method is defined. For slice operations involving extended three-item slice notation, or in the absence of the slice method, __getitem__, __setitem__, or __delitem__ is called instead, with a slice object as its argument.

```
__getslice__(self, low, high)
```
> Invoked on self[low:high] for sequence slicing. This format is considered deprecated as of Python 2.0. If no __getslice__ is found, or if an extended three-item slice is used, then a *slice object* is created and is passed to the __getitem__ method.

```
__setslice__(self, low, high, seq)
```
> Invoked on self[low:high]=seq for sequence slice assignment.

```
__delslice__(self, low, high)
```
> Invoked on del self[low:high] for sequence slice deletion.

For Numbers (Binary Operators)

Basic binary methods

```
__add__(self, other)
```
> Invoked on self + other for numeric addition, or sequence concatenation.

```
__sub__(self, other)
```
> Invoked on self - other.

```
__mul__(self, other)
```
> Invoked on self * other for numeric multiplication, or sequence repetition.

__div__(self, other)
  Invoked on self / other for classic division (integer / truncates).

__floordiv__(self, other)
  Invoked on self // other for truncating (always) division.

__truediv__(self, other)
  Invoked on self / other for true division (optional in Version 2.2, standard in Version 3.0).

__mod__(self, other)
  Invoked on self % other.

__divmod__(self, other)
  Invoked on divmod(self, other).

__pow__(self, other [, modulo])
  Invoked on pow(self, other [, modulo]) and self ** other.

__lshift__(self, other)
  Invoked on self << other.

__rshift__(self, other)
  Invoked on self >> other.

__and__(self, other)
  Invoked on self & other.

__xor__(self, other)
  Invoked on self ^ other.

__or__(self, other)
  Invoked on self | other.

Right-side binary methods

```
__radd__(self, other)
__rsub__(self, other)
__rmul__(self, other)
__rdiv__(self, other)
__rfloordiv__(self, other)
__rtruediv__(self, other)
__rmod__(self, other)
__rdivmod__(self, other)
__rpow__(self, other)
__rlshift__(self, other)
__rrshift__(self, other)
__rand__(self, other)
__rxor__(self, other)
__ror__(self, other)
```

These are right-side operator methods. Binary operator methods have a right-side variant that starts with an r prefix; e.g., __add__ and __radd__. Right-side variants have the same argument lists, but self is on the right side of the operator. For instance, self + other calls self.__add__ (other), but other + self invokes self.__radd__(other).

The r right-side method is called only when the instance is on the right and the left operand is not an instance of a class that overloads the operation:

instance + noninstance runs __add__

instance + instance runs __add__

noninstance + instance runs __radd__

If two different class instances that overload the operation appear, the class on the left is preferred. __radd__ often converts and re-adds to trigger __add__.

Augmented binary methods

```
__iadd__(self, other)
__isub__(self, other)
__imul__(self, other)
__idiv__(self, other)
__ifloordiv__(self, other)
__itruediv__(self, other)
__imod__(self, other)
__ipow__(self, other[, modulo])
__ilshift__(self, other)
__irshift__(self, other)
__iand__(self, other)
__ixor__(self, other)
__ior__(self, other)
```

These are augmented assignment (in-place) methods. Respectively, they are called for the following assignment statement formats: +=, -=, *=, /=, //=, /=, %=, **=, <<=, >>=, &=, ^=, and |=. These methods should attempt to do the operation in-place (modifying self) and return the result (which can be self). If a method is not defined, then the augmented operation falls back on the normal methods. To evaluate X += Y, where X is an instance of a class that has an __iadd__, x.__iadd__(y) is called. Otherwise, __add__ and __radd__ are considered.

For Numbers (Other Operations)

```
__neg__(self)
```
Invoked on -self.

```
__pos__(self)
```
Invoked on +self.

```
__abs__(self)
```
Invoked on abs(self).

```
__invert__(self)
```
Invoked on ~self.

__complex__(self)
    Invoked on complex(self).

__int__(self)
    Invoked on int(self).

__long__(self)
    Invoked on long(self).

__float__(self)
    Invoked on float(self).

__oct__(self)
    Invoked on oct(self). This method returns an octal
    string representation.

__hex__(self)
    Invoked on hex(self). This method returns a hex string
    representation.

__nonzero__(self)
    Invoked on truth-value (otherwise, uses __len__ if
    defined).

__coerce__(self, other)
    Invoked on the mixed-mode arithmetic expression,
    coerce(). This method returns a tuple of (self, other)
    converted to a common type. If __coerce__ is defined, it
    is generally called before any real operator methods are
    tried (e.g., before __add__). It should return a tuple con-
    taining operands converted to a common type (or None if
    it can't convert). See the Python Language Reference
    (*http://www.python.org/doc/*) for more on coercion rules.

Built-in Functions

All built-in names (functions, exceptions, and so on) exist
in the implied outer built-in scope, which corresponds to
the __builtin__ module. Because this scope is always
searched last on name lookups, these functions are always

available in programs without imports. However, their names are not reserved words and might be hidden by assignments to the same name in global or local scopes.

`abs(N)`
Returns the absolute value of a number N.

`apply(func, args [, keys])`
Calls any callable object func (a function, method, class, etc.), passing the positional arguments in tuple args, and the keyword arguments in dictionary keys. It returns the func call result. It is deprecated: the call syntax func(*args, **keys) is preferred.

`basestring()`
The baseclass for normal and Unicode strings (it is useful for isinstance tests).

`bool([x])`
Converts a value to a Boolean, using the standard truth testing procedure. If x is false or omitted, this returns False; otherwise, it returns True. bool is also a class, which is a subclass of int. The class bool cannot be subclassed further. Its only instances are False and True.

`buffer(object [, offset [, size]])`
Returns a new buffer object for a conforming object (see the Python Library Reference). It is deprecated.

`callable(object)`
Returns 1 if object is callable; otherwise, returns 0.

`chr(Int)`
Returns a one-character string whose ASCII code is integer Int.

`classmethod(function)`
Returns a class method for a function. A class method receives the class as an implicit first argument, just like an instance method receives the instance. Use the @classmethod function decorator in Version 2.4 (see the section "The def Statement," earlier in this book).

`cmp(X, Y)`

> Returns a negative integer, zero, or a positive integer to
> designate X < Y, X == Y, or X > Y, respectively.

`coerce(X, Y)`

> Returns a tuple containing the two numeric arguments X
> and Y converted to a common type.

`compile(string, filename, kind)`

> Compiles `string` into a code object. `string` is a Python
> string containing Python program code. `filename` is a
> string used in error messages (and is usually the name of
> the file from which the code was read, or <string> if
> typed interactively). `kind` can be `exec` if `string` contains
> statements; `eval` if `string` is an expression; or `single`,
> which prints the output of an expression statement that
> evaluates to something other than `None`. The resulting
> code object can be executed with `exec` statements or `eval`
> calls.

`complex(real [, imag])`

> Builds a complex number object (it can also be done
> using the J or j suffix: real+imagJ). `imag` defaults to 0.

`delattr(object, name)`

> Deletes the attribute named `name` (a string) from `object`.
> It is similar to `del obj.name`, but `name` is a string, not a
> variable (e.g., `delattr(a,'b')` is like `del a.b`).

`dict([mapping-or-sequence])`

> Returns a new dictionary initialized from a mapping, a
> sequence of key/value pairs, or a set of keyword argu-
> ments. If no argument is given, it returns an empty dic-
> tionary. It is a subclassable type class name.

`dir([object])`

> If no arguments, this returns the list of names in the cur-
> rent local scope (namespace). With any object with
> attributes as an argument, it returns the list of attribute
> names associated with that object. It works on modules,

classes, and class instances, as well as built-in objects with attributes (lists, dictionaries, etc.); it includes inherited attributes, and sorts the result. Use _ _dict_ _ attributes for simple attribute lists.

divmod(X, Y)
Returns a tuple of (X / Y, X % Y).

enumerate(iterable)
Returns an enumerate object. iterable must be a sequence, an iterator, or some other object that supports iteration. The next() method of the iterator returned by enumerate() returns a tuple containing a count (from zero) and the corresponding value obtained from iterating over iterable. It is useful for obtaining an indexed series when both positions and items are required in for loops: (0, seq[0]), (1, seq[1]), (2, seq[2])…. It is new in Version 2.3.

eval(expr [, globals [, locals]])
Evaluates expr, which is assumed to be either a Python string containing a Python expression or a compiled code object. expr is evaluated in the namespaces of the eval call unless the globals and/or locals namespace dictionary arguments are passed. locals defaults to globals if only globals is passed. It returns an expr result. Also see the compile function discussed earlier in this section, and the section "The exec Statement," earlier in this book (for statements).

execfile(filename [, globals [, locals]])
Like eval, but runs all the code in a file whose string name is passed in as filename (instead of an expression). Unlike imports, this does not create a new module object for the file. It returns None. Namespaces for code in filename are as for eval.

file(filename [, mode[, bufsize]])
An alias for the open built-in function, and the subclassable class name of the built-in file type.

`filter(function, sequence)`

Constructs a list from those elements of sequence for which function returns true. function takes one parameter. If function is None, this returns all true items.

`float([X])`

Converts a number or a string X to a floating-point number (or 0.0 if no argument is passed). It is a subclassable type class name.

`frozenset([iterable])`

Returns a *frozen set* object whose elements are taken from iterable. Frozen sets are sets that have no update methods.

`getattr(object, name [, default])`

Returns the value of attribute name (a string) from object. It is similar to object.name, but name is a string, not a variable (e.g., getattr(a,'b') is like a.b). If the named attribute does not exist, default is returned if provided; otherwise, AttributeError is raised.

`globals()`

Returns a dictionary containing the caller's global variables (e.g., the enclosing module's names).

`hasattr(object, name)`

Returns true if object has an attribute called name (a string); false otherwise.

`hash(object)`

Returns the hash value of object (if it has one).

`help([object])`

Invokes the built-in help system. (This function is intended for interactive use.)

`hex(N)`

Converts a number N to a hexadecimal string.

`id(object)`

Returns the unique identity integer of object (i.e., its address in memory).

`__import__(name [,globals [,locals [, fromlist] ]])`

 Imports and returns a module, given its name as a string, not a variable (e.g., mod = __import__("mymod")). It is generally faster than constructing and executing an import statement string with exec. This function is called by import and from statements and can be overridden to customize import operations. The second through fourth arguments have advanced roles (see the Python Library Reference).

`input([prompt])`

 Prints prompt, if given. Then it reads an input line from the *stdin* stream (sys.stdin), evaluates it as Python code, and returns the result. It is like eval(raw_input(prompt)).

`int(X [, base])`

 Converts a number or a string X to a plain integer. base can be passed only if X is a string; if base is passed as 0, the base is determined by the string contents; otherwise, the value passed for base is used for the base of the conversion. Conversion of floating-point numbers to integers truncates toward 0. It is a subclassable type class name.

`intern(string)`

 Enters string in the table of "interned strings" and returns the interned string. Interned strings are "immortals" and serve as a performance optimization (they can be compared by fast is identity, rather than == equality).

`isinstance(object, classOrType)`

 Returns true if object is an instance of classOrType, or an instance of any subclass thereof. classOrType can also be a tuple of classes and/or types.[*]

---

[*] The second argument can also be a type object in more recent Python releases, making this function useful as an alternative type-testing tool (isinstance(X, Type) versus type(X) is Type comparisons).

---

issubclass(class1, class2)

Returns true if class1 is derived from class2. class2 can also be a tuple of classes.

iter(object [, sentinel])

Returns an iterator object that can be used to step through items in object. Iterator objects returned have a next() method that returns the next item or raises StopIteration to end the progression. If one argument, object is assumed to provide its own iterator or be a sequence (normal case); if two arguments, object is a callable that is called until it returns sentinel. It can be overloaded in classes with __iter__; and it can be automatically called by Python in all iteration contexts. It is new in Version 2.2.

len(object)

Returns the number of items (length) in a collection object. It works on sequences and mappings.

list(sequence)

A converter: it returns a new list containing all the items in any sequence object. If sequence is already a list, it returns a copy of it. It is a subclassable type class name.

locals()

Returns a dictionary containing the local variables of the caller (with one *key*:*value* entry per local).

long(X [, base])

Converts a number or a string X to a long integer. base can be passed only if X is a string. If 0, the base is determined by the string contents; otherwise, it is used for the base of the conversion. It is a subclassable type class name.

map(function, seq [, seq]*)

Applies function to every item of any sequence seq and returns a list of the collected results. For example, map(abs, (1, -2)) returns [1, 2]. If additional sequence

---

arguments are passed, function must take that many arguments, and it is passed one item from each sequence on every call. If function is None, map collects all the items into a result list. If sequences differ in length, all are padded to the length of the longest, with Nones.

max(S [, arg]*)

With a single argument S, returns the largest item of a nonempty sequence (e.g., string, tuple, and list). With more than one argument, it returns the largest of the arguments.

min(S [, arg]*)

With a single argument S, returns the smallest item of a nonempty sequence (e.g., string, tuple, list). With more than one argument, it returns the smallest of the arguments.

object()

Returns a new featureless object. It is a base for all new style classes.

oct(N)

Converts a number N to an octal string.

open(filename [, mode, [bufsize]])

Synonymous with file(), this returns a new file object, connected to the external file named filename (a string). The filename is mapped to the current working directory, unless the filename string includes a directory prefix. The first two arguments are the same as those for C's stdio fopen function, and the file is managed by the "stdio" system.

mode defaults to 'r' if omitted, but can be 'r' for input; 'w' for output; 'a' for append; and 'rb', 'wb', or 'ab' for binary files (to suppress line-end conversions). On most systems, most of these can also have a + appended to open in input/output updates mode (e.g., 'r+' to read/write, and 'w+' to read/write but initialize the file to empty).

`bufsize` defaults to an implementation-dependent value, but can be 0 for unbuffered, 1 for line-buffered, negative for system-default, or a given specific size. Buffered data transfers might not be immediately fulfilled (use `flush` methods to force).

`ord(C)`

Returns an integer ASCII value of a one-character string `C` (or the Unicode code point, if `C` is a one-character Unicode string).

`pow(X, Y [, Z])`

Returns `X` to power `Y` [modulo `Z`]. It is similar to the `**` expression operator.

`property([fget[, fset[, fdel[, doc]]]])`

Returns a property attribute for new-style classes (classes that derive from `object`). `fget` is a function for getting an attribute value, `fset` is a function for setting, and `fdel` is a function for deleting.

`range([start,] stop [, step])`

Returns a list of successive integers between `start` and `stop`. With one argument, it returns integers from zero through `stop-1`. With two arguments, it returns integers from `start` through `stop-1`. With three arguments, it returns integers from `start` through `stop-1`, adding `step` to each predecessor in the result. `start`, `step` default to 0, 1. `range(0,20,2)` is a list of even integers from 0 through 18. It is often used to generate offset lists for `for` loops.

`raw_input([prompt])`

Prints a `prompt` string if given, then reads a line from the *stdin* input stream (`sys.stdin`) and returns it as a string. It strips the trailing \n at the end of the line and raises `EOFError` at the end of the *stdin* stream. On platforms where GNU readline is supported, `raw_input()` uses it (as does `input()`).

reduce(func, sequence [, init])

　　Applies the two-argument function func to successive items from sequence, so as to reduce the list to a single value. If init is given, it is prepended to sequence.

reload(module)

　　Reloads, re-parses, and re-executes an already imported module in the module's current namespace. Re-execution replaces prior values of the module's attributes in-place. module must reference an existing module object; it is not a new name or a string. This is useful in interactive mode if you want to reload a module after fixing it, without restarting Python. It returns the module object.

repr(object)

　　Returns a string containing a printable, and potentially parseable, representation of any object. It is equivalent to `object` (back quotes expression).

round(X [, N])

　　Returns the floating-point value X rounded to N digits after the decimal point. N defaults to zero.

set([iterable])

　　Returns a set whose elements are taken from iterable. The elements must be immutable. To represent sets of sets, the inner sets should be frozenset objects. If iterable is not specified, this returns a new empty set. See the section "Sets," earlier in this book. This is new in Version 2.4.

setattr(object, name, value)

　　Assigns value to the attribute name (a string) in object. It is like object.name = value, but name is a string, not a variable name (e.g., setattr(a,'b',c) is like a.b=c).

slice([start ,] stop [, step])

　　Returns a slice object representing a range, with read-only attributes start, stop, and step, any of which can be None. Arguments are the same as for range.

sorted(iterable [, cmp[, key[, reverse]]]))
> Returns a new sorted list from the items in iterable. The optional arguments cmp, key, and reverse have the same meaning as those for the list.sort() method. It is useful in for loops, to avoid splitting sort calls out to separate statements due to None returns. It is new in Version 2.4.

staticmethod(function)
> Returns a static method for function. A static method does not receive an implicit first argument, and so is useful for processing class attributes that span instances. Use the @staticmethod function decorator in Version 2.4 (see the section "The def Statement," earlier in this book).

str([object])
> Returns a string containing the printable representation of object. It is a subclassable type class name.

sum(sequence [, start])
> Sums start and the items of a sequence, from left to right, and returns the total. start defaults to 0. The sequence's items are normally numbers, and are not allowed to be strings (to concatenate a sequence of strings, use ''.join(sequence)).

super(type [, object-or-type])
> Returns the superclass of type. If the second argument is omitted, the super object returned is unbound. If the second argument is an object, isinstance(obj, type) must be true. If the second argument is a type, issubclass(type2, type) must be true. This works only for new-style classes.

tuple(sequence)
> A converter: it returns a new tuple with the same elements as any sequence passed in. If sequence is already a tuple, it is returned directly (not a copy). It is a subclassable type class name.

`type(object)`

> Returns a type object representing the type of object. It is useful for type-testing in `if` statements (e.g., `if type(X)==type([]):`). See also module types for preset objects to compare result to (e.g., `types.ListType`), and `isinstance`, earlier in this section.

`unichr(i)`

> Returns the Unicode string of one character whose Unicode code is the integer i (e.g., `unichr(97)` returns the string `u'a'`). This is the inverse of `ord` for Unicode strings. The argument must be in range 0...65535 inclusive, or `ValueError` is raised.

`unicode(string [, encoding [, errors]])`

> Decodes `string` using the codec for encoding. Error handling is done according to errors. The default behavior is to decode UTF-8 in strict mode, meaning that encoding errors raise `ValueError`. See also the codecs module in the Python Library Reference.

`vars([object])`

> Without arguments, returns a dictionary containing the current local scope's names. With a module, class, or class instance object as an argument, it returns a dictionary corresponding to object's attribute namespace (i.e., its `__dict__`). It is useful for % string formatting.

`xrange([start,] stop [, step])`

> Like range, but doesn't actually store the entire list all at once (rather, it generates one integer at a time). It is good to use in `for` loops when there is a big range and little memory. It optimizes space, but generally has no speed benefit.

`zip(seq [, seq]*)`

> Returns a list of tuples, where each ith tuple contains the ith element from each of the argument sequences seq. For example, `zip('ab', 'cd')` returns `[('a', 'c'), ('b', 'd')]`. At least one sequence is required, or a `TypeError` is

raised. The result list is truncated to the length of the shortest argument sequence. When there are multiple argument sequences of the same length, zip is similar to map with a first argument of None. With a single sequence argument, it returns a list of one-tuples.

Built-in Exceptions

This section describes the exceptions that Python might raise during a program's execution. Beginning with Python 1.5, all built-in exceptions are class objects. Prior to 1.5, they were strings. Class exceptions are mostly indistinguishable from strings, unless they are concatenated. Built-in exceptions are available in the module exceptions; this module never needs to be imported explicitly because the exception names are provided in the built-in scope namespace. Most built-in exceptions have an associated extra data value with details.

Base Classes (Categories)

Exception
> The root superclass for all exceptions. User-defined exceptions can be derived from this class, but this is not currently enforced or required.

StandardError
> The superclass for all other built-in exceptions except for SystemExit; it is a subclass of the Exception root class.

ArithmeticError
> The superclass for OverflowError, ZeroDivisionError, and FloatingPointError; it is a subclass of StandardError.

LookupError
> The superclass for IndexError and KeyError; it is a subclass of StandardError.

EnvironmentError
> The superclass for exceptions that occur outside Python (IOError, OSError); it is a subclass of StandardError.

Specific Exceptions Raised

AssertionError
 Raised when an assert statement's test is false.

AttributeError
 Raised on attribute reference or assignment failure.

EOFError
 Raised when the immediate end-of-file is hit by input()
 or raw_input().

FloatingPointError
 Raised on floating-point operation failure.

IOError
 Raised on I/O or file-related operation failures.

ImportError
 Raised when an import fails to find a module or
 attribute.

IndexError
 Raised on out-of-range sequence offsets (fetch or assign).

KeyError
 Raised on references to nonexistent mapping keys
 (fetch).

KeyboardInterrupt
 Raised on user entry of the interrupt key (often Ctrl-C).

MemoryError
 Raised on recoverable memory exhaustion.

NameError
 Raised on failures to find a local or global unqualified
 name.

NotImplementedError
 Raised on failures to define expected protocols.

OSError
 Raised on os module errors (its os.error exception).

OverflowError
Raised on excessively large arithmetic operations.

ReferenceError
Raised in weak reference

RuntimeError
A rarely used catch-all.

StopIteration
Raised on the end of progression in iterator objects.

SyntaxError
Raised when parsers encounter a syntax error.

SystemError
Raised on interpreter internal errors (bugs—report them).

SystemExit
Raised on a call to sys.exit( ) (can trap and ignore).

TypeError
Raised when passing inappropriate types to built-in operations.

UnboundLocalError
Raised on references to local name that have not been assigned.

UnicodeError
Raised on Unicode-related encoding or decoding errors; a superclass category.

UnicodeEncodeError
UnicodeDecodeError
UnicodeTrabslateError
Raised on Unicode-related processing errors.

ValueError
Raised on argument errors not covered by TypeError or others.

`WindowsError`
    Raised on Windows-specific errors.

`ZeroDivisionError`
    Raised on division or modulus operations with 0 on the right.

Warning Category Exceptions

The following exceptions are used as warning categories.

`Warning`
    The base class for all of the following warning categories; it is a subclass of `Exception`.

`UserWarning`
    The base class for warnings generated by user code.

`PendingDeprecationWarning`
    The base class for warnings about features that will be deprecated in the future.

`DeprecationWarning`
    The base class for warnings about deprecated features.

`SyntaxWarning`
    The base class for warnings about dubious syntax.

`RuntimeWarning`
    The base class for warnings about dubious runtime behavior.

`FutureWarning`
    The base class for warnings about constructs that will change semantically in the future.

Warnings Framework

Warnings are issued when future language changes might break existing code in a future Python release. You can use the warnings framework to issue warnings by calling the `warnings.warn` function:

```
warnings.warn("feature X no longer supported")
```

In addition, you can add filters to disable certain warnings. You can apply a regular expression pattern to a message or module name to suppress warnings with varying degrees of generality. For example, you can suppress a warning about the use of the deprecated regex module by calling:

```
import warnings
warnings.filterwarnings(action = 'ignore',
                        message='.*regex module*',
                        category=DeprecationWarning,
                        module = '__main__')
```

This adds a filter that affects only warnings of the class `DeprecationWarning` triggered in the __main__ module, applies a regular expression to match only the message that names the regex module being deprecated, and causes such warnings to be ignored. Warnings can be printed only once, printed every time the offending code is executed, or turned into exceptions that will cause the program to stop (unless the exceptions are caught). See the `warnings` module documentation in Version 2.1 and later for more information. See also the -W argument in the section "Command-Line Options," earlier in this book.

Built-in Attributes

Some objects export special attributes that are predefined by Python.[*] The following is a partial list because many types have unique attributes all their own; see the entries for specific types in the Python Library Reference.

---

[*] As of Python 2.1, you can also attach arbitrary user-defined attributes to *function* objects, simply by assigning them values.

`X.__dict__`
>   Dictionary used to store object X's writable attributes.

`I.__methods__`
>   List of instance object I's methods (name strings); it is
>   available on many built-in types.[*]

`I.__members__`
>   List of instance object I's data attributes (name strings);
>   it is available on many built-in types.

`I.__class__`
>   Class object from which instance I was generated. In
>   Version 2.2, this also applies to object types; most
>   objects will have a `__class__` attribute (e.g., `[].__class__ == list == type([])`).

`C.__bases__`
>   Tuple of class C's base classes, as listed in C's class state-
>   ment header.

`X.__name__`
>   Object X's name as a string; for classes, the name in the
>   statement header; for modules, the name as used in
>   imports, or `"__main__"` for the module at the top level of
>   a program (e.g., the main file run to launch a program).

Built-in Modules

Built-in modules are always available but must be imported
to be used in client modules. To access them, use one of
these formats:

- `import module`, and fetch attribute names (`module.name`)
- `from module import name`, and use module names unqualified (`name`)
- `from module import *`, and use module names unqualified
  (`name`)

---

[*] `_methods__` and `__members__` are deprecated since Version 2.2; use the
built-in `dir()` function instead.

For instance, to use name `argv` in the sys module, either use `import sys` and name `sys.argv`, or use `from sys import argv` and name `argv`.

There are hundreds of built-in modules; the next sections document commonly used names in commonly used modules. Listed export names followed by parentheses are functions that must be called; others are simple attributes (i.e., variable names in modules).

The sys Module

The sys module contains interpreter-related exports. It also provides access to some environment components, such as the command line, standard streams, and so on.

argv
  Command-line argument strings list: [command, arguments...]. Like C's argv array.

byteorder
  Indicates the native byte-order (e.g., big for big-endian).

builtin_module_names
  Tuple of string names of C modules compiled into this Python interpreter.

copyright
  String containing the Python interpreter copyright.

dllhandle
  Python DLL integer handle; Windows only (see the Python Library Reference).

displayhook(func)
  Called by Python to display results in interactive sessions; assign sys.displayhook to a one-argument function to customize output.

__displayhook__
  Original value of displayhook (for restores).

`excepthook(type, value, traceback)`
> Called by Python to display exception details to stderr; assign sys.excepthook to a three-argument function to customize exception displays.

`__excepthook__`
> Original value of excepthook (for restores).

`exc_info()`
> Returns tuple of three values describing the exception currently being handled: (type, value, traceback). Specific to current thread. Subsumes exc_type, exc_value, and exc_traceback in Python 1.5 and later. See the traceback module in the Python Library Reference for processing traceback objects.

`exc_clear()`
> Clears all exception information in current thread (rarely needed).

`exc_type`
> Type of exception being handled (when an exception has been raised). Not thread-specific, deprecated.

`exc_value`
> Exception's parameter (second argument to raise). Not thread-specific, deprecated.

`exc_traceback`
> Exception's traceback object. Not thread-specific, deprecated.

`exec_prefix`
> Assign to a string giving the site-specific directory prefix where the platform-dependent Python files are installed; defaults to */usr/local* or a build-time argument. Use this to locate shared library modules (in *<exec_prefix>/lib/ python<version>/lib-dynload*) and configuration files.

executable

String giving the file pathname of the Python interpreter program running the caller.

exit([N])

Exits from a Python process with status N (default 0) by raising a SystemExit built-in exception (can be caught in a try statement and ignored). See also the os._exit() function (in the section "The os System Module," later in this book), which exits immediately without exception processing (useful in child processes after an os.fork()).

exitfunc

May assign a no-argument function to be called on exit.[*]

getcheckinterval()

Returns the interpreter's "check interval"; see setcheckinterval, later in this list.

getdefaultencoding()

Returns the name of the current default string encoding used by the Unicode implementation.

getrefcount(object)

Returns object's current reference count value (+1 for the call's argument).

getrecursionlimit()

Returns the maximum depth limit of the Python call stack; see also setrecursionlimit, later in this list.

_getframe([depth])

Returns a frame object from the Python call stack (see the Python Library Reference).

hexversion

Python version number, encoded as a single integer (viewed best with the hex built-in function). Increases with each new release.

---

[*] exitfunc is somewhat deprecated as of Version 2.0; use the atexit module instead.

`last_type`
`last_value`
`last_traceback`
> Type, value, and traceback object of last uncaught exception (mostly for postmortem debugging).

`maxint`
> Maximum positive value of plain integer on platform.

`modules`
> Dictionary of modules that are already loaded; there is one `name:object` entry per module. Writable (for example, `del sys.modules['name']` forces a module to be reloaded on next import).

`path`
> List of strings specifying module import search path. Initialized from `PYTHONPATH` shell variable, *.pth* path files, and any installation-dependent defaults. Writable (e.g., `sys.path.append('C:\\dir')` adds a directory to the search path within a script).
>
> The first item, `path[0]`, is the directory containing the script that was used to invoke the Python interpreter. If the script directory is not available (e.g., if the interpreter is invoked interactively or if the script is read from standard input), `path[0]` is the empty string, which directs Python to search modules in the current working directory first. The script directory is inserted before the entries inserted from `PYTHONPATH`.

`platform`
> String identifying the system on which Python is running: e.g., `'sunos5'`, `'linux2'`, `'win32'`, `'PalmOS3'`. Useful for tests in platform-dependent code. Hint: `'win32'` means all current flavors of Windows, or test as `sys.platform[:3]=='win'`.

`prefix`
> Assign to a string giving the site-specific directory prefix, where platform-independent Python files are installed;

defaults to */usr/local* or a build-time argument. Python library modules are installed in the directory *<prefix>/lib/python<version>*; platform-independent header files are stored in *<prefix>/include/python<version>*.

ps1

String specifying primary prompt in interactive mode; defaults to >>> unless assigned.

ps2

String specifying secondary prompt for compound statement continuations, in interactive mode; defaults to ... unless assigned.

setcheckinterval(reps)

Call to set how often the interpreter checks for periodic tasks (e.g., thread switches, signal handlers) to reps. Measured in virtual machine instructions (default is 10). In general, a Python statement translates to multiple virtual machine instructions. Lower values maximize thread responsiveness but also maximize thread switch overhead.

setdefaultencoding(name)

Call to set the current default string encoding used by the Unicode implementation. New in Version 2.0, and somewhat experimental.

setprofile(func)

Call to set the system profile function to func: the profiler's "hook" (not run for each line). See the Python Library Reference for details.

setrecursionlimit(depth)

Call to set maximum depth of the Python call stack to depth. This limit prevents infinite recursion from causing an overflow of the C stack and crashing Python.

settrace(func)

Call to set the system trace function to func: the "hook" used by debuggers, etc. See the Python Library Reference for details.

stdin
> Standard input stream: a preopened file object. Can be assigned to any object with read methods to reset input within a script (e.g., sys.stdin=MyObj()). Used for interpreter input, including raw_input() and input() built-in function calls.

stdout
> Standard output stream: a preopened file object. Can be assigned to any object with write methods to reset output within a script (e.g., sys.stdout=open('log', 'a')). Used for some prompts and the print statement.

stderr
> Standard error stream: a preopened file object. Can be assigned to any object with write methods to reset stderr within a script (e.g., sys.stderr=wrappedsocket). Used for interpreter prompts/errors.

__stdin__
__stdout__
__stderr__
> Original values of stdin, stderr, and stdout at program start (e.g., for restores as a last resort; normally, when assigning to sys.stdout, etc., save the old value and restore it in a finally clause).

tracebacklimit
> Maximum number of traceback levels to print; defaults to 1,000.

version
> String containing the version number of the Python interpreter.

version_info
> Tuple containing five version identification components (see the Python Library Reference).

---

winver
>   Version number used to form registry keys on Windows
>   platforms (available only on Windows; see the Python
>   Library Reference).

The string Module

The string module defines constants and variables for processing string objects. See also the section "Strings," earlier in this book, for a discussion of the string template substitution tools Template and SafeTemplate defined in this module.

Module Functions

As of Python 2.0, most functions in this module are also available as methods of string objects, and method-based calls are preferred and are more efficient. See the section "Strings," earlier in this book, for more details and a list of all available string methods not repeated here. Only items unique to the string module are listed in this section.

atof(s)
atoi(s [, base])
atol(s [, base])
>   Severely deprecated string-to-number converters. Use
>   built-in functions float(), int(), and long() instead (see
>   the section "Built-in Functions," earlier in this book).

capwords(s)
>   Split the argument into words using split, capitalize
>   each word using capitalize, and join the capitalized
>   words using join. Replaces runs of whitespace characters by a single space, and removes leading and trailing
>   whitespace.

maketrans(from, to)

Return a translation table suitable for passing to translate or regex.compile, that will map each character in from into the character at the same position in to; from and to must have the same length.

Template, SafeTemplate

String template substitution (see the section "Strings," earlier in this book).

Constants

ascii_letters

The string ascii_lowercase + ascii_uppercase.

ascii_lowercase

The string 'abcdefghijklmnopqrstuvwxyz'; not locale-dependent and will not change.

ascii_uppercase

The string 'ABCDEFGHIJKLMNOPQRSTUVWXYZ'; not locale-dependent and will not change.

digits

The string '0123456789'.

hexdigits

The string '0123456789abcdefABCDEF'.

letters

Concatenation of the strings lowercase and uppercase.

lowercase

Usually, the string 'abcdefghijklmnopqrstuvwxyz'.[*]

octdigits

The string '01234567'.

---

[*] lowercase, uppercase, whitespace, etc., are dependent on the current 8-bit locale; the examples shown are for 7-bit U.S. ASCII.

printable

    Combination of digits, letters, punctuation, and whitespace.

punctuation

    String of characters that are considered punctuation characters.

uppercase

    Usually `'ABCDEFGHIJKLMNOPQRSTUVWXYZ'`.

whitespace

    String containing space, tab, linefeed, return, formfeed, and vertical tab.

The os System Module

The os module is the primary operating system (OS) services interface. It provides generic operating-system support and a standard, platform-independent OS interface. The os module includes tools for environments, processes, files, shell commands, and much more. It also includes a nested submodule, os.path, which provides a portable interface to directory processing tools.

Scripts that use os and os.path for systems programming are generally portable across most Python platforms. However, some os exports are not available on all platforms (e.g., fork is available on Unix but not Windows). Because the portability of such calls changes over time, consult the Python Library Reference for platform details.

Administrative Tools

Following are some miscellaneous module-related exports.

error

    Known as both os.error and built-in OSError exception. Raised for os module-related errors. The accompanying value is a pair containing the numeric error code from errno and the corresponding string, as would be printed by the C function perror(). See the module errno in the Python Library Reference for names of the error codes defined by the underlying OS.

When exceptions are classes, this exception carries two attributes: errno, the value of the C errno variable; and strerror, the corresponding error message from strerror(). For exceptions that involve a file pathname (e.g., chdir(), unlink()), the exception instance also contains the attribute filename, the filename passed in.

name

Name of OS-specific modules whose names are copied to the top level of os (e.g., posix, nt, dos, mac, os2, ce, or java). See also platform in the section "The sys Module," earlier in this book.

path

Nested module for portable pathname-based utilities. For example, os.path.split is a platform-independent directory name tool that internally uses an appropriate platform-specific call.

Portability Constants

This section describes tools for parsing and building directory and search path strings portably. They are automatically set to the appropriate value for the platform on which a script is running.

curdir

String used to represent current directory (e.g., . for POSIX, : for Macintosh).

pardir

String used to represent parent directory (e.g., .. for POSIX, :: for Macintosh).

sep

String used to separate directories (e.g., / for Unix, \ for Windows, or : for Macintosh).

altsep
> Alternative separator string or None (e.g., / for Windows).

extsep
> The character which separates the base filename from the extension (e.g., .).

pathsep
> Character used to separate search path components, as in the PATH and PYTHONPATH shell variable settings (e.g., ; for Windows, : for Unix).

defpath
> Default search path used by os.exec*p* calls if there is no PATH setting in the shell.

linesep
> String used to terminate lines on current platform (e.g., \n for POSIX, \r for Mac OS, and \r\n for MS-DOS and Windows).

Shell Commands

These functions run programs in the underlying operating system.

system(cmd)
> Executes a command string cmd in a subshell process. Returns the exit status of the spawned process. Unlike popen, does not connect to cmd's standard streams via pipes. Hints: add an & at the end of cmd to run the command in the background on Unix (e.g., os.system('python main.py &')); use a DOS start command to launch programs easily on Windows (e.g., os.system('start file.html')).

startfile(filepathname)
> Starts a file with its associated application. Acts like double-clicking the file in Windows Explorer or giving the filename an argument to a DOS start command (e.g., with os.system('start path')). The file is opened in the

application with which its extension is associated; the call does not wait, and does not generally pop up a DOS console window. Windows only, new in Version 2.0.

popen(cmd [, mode [, bufsize]])

Opens a pipe to or from the shell command string cmd, to send or capture data. Returns an open file object, which can be used to either read from cmd's standard output stream stdout (mode 'r') or write to cmd's standard input stream stdin (mode 'w'). For example, dirlist = os.popen('ls -l *.py').read() gets the output of a Unix ls command.

cmd is any command string you can type at your system's console or shell prompt. mode can be 'r' or 'w' and defaults to 'r'. bufsize is the same as in the built-in open function. cmd runs independently; its exit status is returned by the resulting file object's close method, except that None is returned if exit status is 0 (no errors).

In the popen variants listed next, bufsize is the buffer size for the I/O pipes and mode is the string 'b' or 't', for binary or text transfer modes, respectively. mode defaults to 't'; 'b' is useful on Windows to force the file objects to be opened in binary mode and to suppress automatic linefeed conversions. The popen2 module exports similar calls, but return value order differs.

popen2(cmd [, bufsize [, mode]])

Executes cmd as a subprocess and connects to both its standard input and output streams. Returns a tuple of two file objects: (child_stdin, child_stdout). New in Version 2.0.

popen3(cmd [, bufsize [, mode]])

Executes cmd as a subprocess and connects to all three of its standard streams. Returns the child object's tuple (child_stdin, child_stdout, child_stderr). New in Version 2.0.

popen4(cmd [, bufsize [, mode]])

> Like popen3, but ties stdout and stderr to a single output
> pipe. Returns the file object's tuple: (child_stdin, child_
> stdout_and_stderr). New in Version 2.0.

See also the subprocess module in Version 2.4 and later,
which allows you to spawn new processes, connect to their
input/output/error pipes, and obtain their return codes in
other ways.

Environment Tools

These attributes export execution environment and context.

environ

> The shell environment variable dictionary. os.
> environ['USER'] is the value of variable USER in the shell
> (equivalent to $USER in Unix and %USER% in DOS). Initial-
> ized on program startup. Changes made to os.environ by
> key assignment are exported outside Python using a call
> to C's putenv and are inherited by any processes that are
> later spawned in any way, and any linked-in C code.

putenv(varname, value)

> Sets the shell environment variable named varname to the
> string value. Affects subprocesses started with system,
> popen, spawnv, or fork and execv. Assignment to os.
> environ keys automatically calls putenv (but putenv calls
> don't update environ).

getcwd()

> Returns the current working directory name as a string.

chdir(path)

> Changes the current working directory for this process to
> path, a directory name string. Future file operations are
> relative to the new current working directory.

strerror(code)

> Returns an error message corresponding to code.

times()
> Returns a five-tuple containing elapsed CPU time information for the calling process in floating-point seconds: (*user-time*, *system-time*, *child-user-time*, *child-system-time*, *elapsed-real-time*). Also see the section "The time Module," later in this book.

tmpfile()
> Returns a new file object opened in update mode ('w+'). The file has no directory entries associated with it and will be automatically deleted once there are no file descriptors for the file.

umask(mask)
> Sets the numeric umask to mask and returns the prior value.

uname()
> Returns OS name tuple of strings: (*systemname*, *nodename*, *release*, *version*, *machine*).

confstr(name)
confstr_names
sysconf(name)
sysconf_names
> System configuration value access (see the Python Library Reference for details).

File Descriptor Tools

The following functions process files by their descriptors (fd is a file-descriptor integer). os module descriptor-based files are meant for low-level file tasks and are not the same as stdio file objects returned by the built-in open function (though os.fdopen and the file object fileno method convert between the two). File objects, not descriptors, should normally be used for most file processing.

close(fd)
> Closes file descriptor fd (not a file object).

`dup(fd)`

    Returns duplicate of file descriptor `fd`.

`dup2(fd, fd2)`

    Copies file descriptor `fd` to `fd2` (close `fd2` first if open).

`fdopen(fd [, mode [, bufsize]])`

    Returns a built-in file object (`stdio`) connected to file descriptor `fd` (an integer). `mode` and `bufsize` have the same meaning as in the built-in `open` function (see the section "Built-in Functions," earlier in this book). A conversion from descriptor-based files to file objects is normally created by the built-in `open` function. Hint: use `fileobj.fileno` to convert a file object to a descriptor.

`fstat(fd)`

    Returns status for file descriptor `fd` (like `stat`).

`ftruncate(fd, length)`

    Truncates the file corresponding to file descriptor `fd` so that it is at most `length` bytes in size.

`isatty(fd)`

    Returns 1 if file descriptor `fd` is open and connected to a tty(-like) device.

`lseek(fd, pos, how)`

    Sets the current position of file descriptor `fd` to `pos` (for random access). `how` can be 0 to set the position relative to the start of the file, 1 to set it relative to the current position, or 2 to set it relative to the end.

`open(filename, flags [, mode])`

    Opens a file descriptor-based file and returns the file descriptor (an integer, not an `stdio` file object). Intended for low-level file tasks only; not the same as the built-in `open` function. `mode` defaults to 0777 (octal), and the current `umask` value is first masked out. `flag` is a bitmask: use `|` to combine flag constants defined in the `os` module (see Table 18).

```
pipe()
```
See the section "Process Control," later in this book.

```
read(fd, n)
```
Reads at most n bytes from file descriptor fd and returns those bytes as a string.

```
write(fd, str)
```
Writes all bytes in string str to file descriptor fd.

```
fpathconf(fd, infoname)
fstatvfs(fd)
ttyname(fd)
openpty()
```
Consult the Python Library Reference or Unix manpages for details.

Table 18. Or-able flags for os.open

O_APPEND	O_EXCL	O_RDONLY	O_TRUNC
O_BINARY	O_NDELAY	O_RDWR	O_WRONLY
O_CREAT	O_NOCTTY	O_RSYNC	
O_DSYNC	O_NONBLOCK	O_SYNC	

File Pathname Tools

The following functions process files by their pathnames (path is a string pathname of a file). See also the section "The os.path Module," later in this book.

```
chdir(path)
getcwd()
```
See the section "Environment Tools," earlier in this book.

```
chmod(path, mode)
```
Changes mode of file path to numeric mode.

```
chown(path, uid, gid)
```
Changes owner/group IDs of path to numeric uid/gid.

---

link(srcpath, dstpath)
   Creates a hard link to file src, named dst.

listdir(path)
   Returns a list of names of all the entries in the directory path. A fast and portable alternative to the glob module and to running shell listing commands with os.popen.

lstat(path)
   Like stat, but does not follow symbolic links.

mkfifo(path [, mode])
   Creates a *FIFO* (a named pipe) identified by string path with numeric mode mode (but does not open it). The default mode is 0666 (octal). The current umask value is first masked out from the mode. FIFOs are pipes that live in the filesystem and can be opened and processed like regular files. FIFOs exist until deleted.

mkdir(path [, mode])
   Makes a directory called path, with the given mode. The default mode is 777 (octal).

makedirs(path [, mode])
   Recursive directory-creation function. Like mkdir, but makes all intermediate-level directories needed to contain the leaf directory. Throws an exception if the leaf directory already exists or cannot be created. mode defaults to 0777 (octal).

readlink(path)
   Returns the path referenced by a symbolic link path.

remove(path)
unlink(path)
   Removes (deletes) the file named path. remove is identical to unlink. See rmdir and removedirs, discussed in this list, for removing directories.

removedirs(path)
   Recursive directory-removal function. Similar to rmdir, but if the leaf directory is successfully removed, then

directories corresponding to the rightmost path segments will be pruned away until either the whole path is consumed or an error is raised. Throws an exception if the leaf directory could not be removed.

rename(srcpath, dstpath)
Renames (moves) file src to name dst.

renames(oldpath, newpath)
Recursive directory- or file-renaming function. Like rename, but creation of any intermediate directories needed to make the new pathname good is attempted first. After the rename, directories corresponding to the rightmost path segments of the old name will be pruned away using removedirs.

rmdir(path)
Removes (deletes) a directory named path.

stat(path)
Runs stat system call for path; returns a tuple of integers with low-level file information (whose items are defined and processed by tools in module stat).

symlink(srcpath, dstpath)
Creates a symbolic link to file src, called dst.

tempnam([dir [, prefix]])
Returns a unique pathname reasonable for creating a temporary file: an absolute path that names a potential directory entry in the directory dir (or in a common location for temporary files if dir is either omitted or None). prefix provides a short prefix to the filename. No automatic creation or cleanup is provided.

tmpnam( )
Returns a unique pathname reasonable for creating a temporary file: an absolute path that names a potential directory entry in a common location for temporary files. No automatic creation or cleanup is provided.

TMP_MAX
> The maximum number of unique names that tmpnam generates before reusing names.

utime(path, (atime, mtime))
> Sets file path access and modification times.

access(path, mode)
statvfs(path)
pathconf(path, infoname)
pathconf_names
> Consult the Python Library Reference or Unix manpages for details.

walk(top [, topdown=True [, onerror=None]]))
> Generates the filenames in a directory tree by walking the tree either top-down or bottom-up. For each directory in the tree rooted at directory top (including top itself), yields a three-tuple (dirpath, dirnames, filenames). dirpath is a string, the path to the directory. dirnames is a list of the names of the subdirectories in dirpath (excluding . and ..). filenames is a list of the names of the non-directory files in dirpath. Note that the names in the lists do not contain path components. To get a full path (which begins with top) to a file or directory in dirpath, do os.path.join(dirpath, name).
>
> If optional argument topdown is true or not specified, the triple for a directory is generated before the triples for any of its subdirectories (directories are generated top-down). If topdown is false, the triple for a directory is generated after the triples for all its subdirectories (directories are generated bottom-up). If optional onerror is specified, it should be a function, which will be called with one argument, an os.error instance. See also os.path.walk later in this book, in the section "The os.path Module."

Process Control

The following functions are used to create and manage processes and programs. Refer also to the "Shell Commands"

section, earlier in this book, for other ways to start programs
and files.

abort()
> Sends a SIGABRT signal to the current process. On Unix,
> the default behavior is to produce a core dump; on Win-
> dows, the process immediately returns exit code 3.

execl(path, arg0, arg1,...)
> Equivalent to execv(path, (arg0, arg1,...)).

execle(path, arg0, arg1,..., env)
> Equivalent to execve(path, (arg0, arg1,...), env).

execlp(path, arg0, arg1,...)
> Equivalent to execvp(path, (arg0, arg1,...)).

execve(path, args, env)
> Like execv, but the env dictionary replaces the shell vari-
> able environment. env must map strings to strings.

execvp(path, args)
> Like execv(path, args), but duplicates the shell's actions
> in searching for an executable file in a list of directories.
> The directory list is obtained from os.environ['PATH'].

execvpe(path, args, env)
> A cross between execve and execvp. The directory list is
> obtained from os.environ['PATH'].

execv(path, args)
> Executes the executable file path with the command-line
> argument args, replacing the current program in this pro-
> cess (the Python interpreter). args can be a tuple or a list
> of strings, and it starts with the executable's name by
> convention (argv[0]). This function call never returns,
> unless an error occurs while starting the new program.

_exit(n)
> Exits the process immediately with status n, without per-
> forming cleanup. Normally used only in a child process
> after a fork; the standard way to exit is to call sys.
> exit(n).

`fork()`

> Spawns a child process (a virtual copy of the calling process, running in parallel); returns 0 in the child and the new child's process ID in the parent.

`getpid()`
`getppid()`

> Returns the process ID of the current (calling) process; `getppid()` returns the parent process ID.

`getuid()`
`geteuid()`

> Returns the process's user ID; `geteuid` returns the effective user ID.

`kill(pid, sig)`

> Kills the process with ID `pid` by sending signal `sig`.

`mkfifo(path [, mode])`

> See the previous section, "File Pathname Tools" (files used for process synchronization).

`nice(increment)`

> Adds `increment` to process's "niceness" (i.e., lowers its CPU priority).

`pipe()`

> Returns a tuple of file descriptors (`rfd`, `wfd`) for reading and writing a new anonymous (unnamed) pipe. Used for cross-process communication.

`plock(op)`

> Locks program segments into memory. `op` (defined in `<sys./lock.h>`) determines which segments are locked.

`spawnv(mode, path, args)`

> Executes program `path` in a new process, passing the arguments specified in `args` as a command line. `args` can be a list or a tuple. `mode` is a magic operational constant made from the following names: `P_WAIT`, `P_NOWAIT`, `P_NOWAITO`, `P_OVERLAY`, and `P_DETACH`. On Windows, roughly equivalent to a fork+execv combination (fork is not yet available on Windows, though popen and system are).

```
spawnve(mode, path, args, env)
```
Like spawnv, but passes the contents of mapping env as the spawned program's shell environment.

```
wait()
```
Waits for completion of a child process. Returns a tuple with child's ID and exit status.

```
waitpid(pid, options)
```
Waits for child process with ID pid to complete. options is 0 for normal use, or os.WNOHANG to avoid hanging if no child status is available. If pid is 0, the request applies to any child in the process group of the current process. See also the process exit status-check functions documented in the Python Library Reference (e.g., WEXITSTATUS(*status*) to extract the exit code).

```
ctermid()
tcgetpgrp(fd)
tcsetpgrp(fd, pg)
setgid(id)
setegid(id)
setpgrp()
setpgid(pid, pgrp)
setreuid(ruid, euid)
setregid(rgid, egid)
setsid()
setuid(id)
seteuid(id)
getgid()
getpgrp()
getegid()
getgroups()
forkpty()
```
Consult the Python Library Reference or Unix manpages for details.

The os.path Module

The os.path module provides additional file directory path-name-related services and portability tools. This is a nested module: its names are nested in the os module within the submodule os.path (e.g., the exists function is obtained by importing os and using os.path.exists). Most functions in this module take an argument path, the string directory pathname of a file (e.g., "C:\dir1\spam.txt"). Directory paths are generally coded per the platform's conventions and are mapped to the current working directory if lacking a directory prefix. Hint: forward slashes usually work as directory separators on all platforms.

abspath(path)

> Returns a normalized absolute version of path. On most platforms, this is equivalent to normpath(join(os.getcwd(), path)).

basename(path)

> Same as second half of pair returned by split(path).

commonprefix(list)

> Returns longest path prefix (character by character) that is a prefix of all paths in list.

dirname(path)

> Same as first half of pair returned by split(path).

exists(path)

> True if string path is the name of an existing file path.

expanduser(path)

> Returns string that is path with embedded ~ username expansion done.

expandvars(path)

> Returns string that is path with embedded $ environment variables expanded.

getatime(path)

Returns time of last access of path (seconds since the epoch).

getmtime(path)

Returns time of last modification of path (seconds since the epoch).

getsize(path)

Returns size, in bytes, of file path.

isabs(path)

True if string path is an absolute path.

isfile(path)

True if string path is a regular file.

isdir(path)

True if string path is a directory.

islink(path)

True if string path is a symbolic link.

ismount(path)

True if string path is a mount point.

join(path1 [, path2 [, ...]])

Joins one or more path components intelligently (using platform-specific separator conventions between each part).

normcase(path)

Normalizes case of a pathname. Has no effect on Unix; on case-insensitive filesystems, converts to lowercase; on Windows, also converts / to \.

normpath(path)

Normalizes a pathname. Collapses redundant separators and up-level references; on Windows, converts / to \.

realpath(path)

> Returns the canonical path of the specified filename, eliminating any symbolic links encountered in the path.

samefile(path1, path2)

> Returns true if both pathname arguments refer to the same file or directory.

sameopenfile(fp1, fp2)

> Returns true if both file objects refer to the same file.

samestat(stat1, stat2)

> Returns true if both stat tuples refer to the same file.

split(path)

> Splits path into (head, tail), where tail is the last pathname component and head is everything leading up to tail. Same as tuple (dirname(path), basename(path)).

splitdrive(path)

> Splits path into a pair ('drive:', tail) (on Windows).

splitext(path)

> Splits path into (root, ext), where the last component of root contains no . and ext is empty or starts with a ..

walk(path, visitor, data)

> Callback-based directory tree walker. Performs a recursive directory traversal. During the traversal, calls function visitor with arguments (data, dirname, filesindir) for each directory and subdirectory in the directory tree rooted at path (including path itself if it is a directory). The argument dirname names the visited directory; the argument filesindir is a list of all the filenames in directory dirname; the argument data is the data object passed to the walk call. visitor can modify filesindir to influence the set of directories visited below dirname (e.g., delete names to prune tree). See also the os.path.walk generator earlier in this book, in the section "File Pathname Tools."

The re Pattern-Matching Module

The re module is the standard regular expression-matching interface. Regular expression (RE) patterns are specified as strings. This module must be imported.[*]

Module Functions

compile(pattern [, flags])

Compile an RE pattern string into a regular expression object, for later matching. flags (combinable by bitwise | operator) include the following:

I *or* IGNORECASE *or* (?i)
Case-insensitive matching.

L *or* LOCALE *or* (?L)
Makes \w, \W, \b, \B, \s, \S, \d, and \D dependent on the current 8-bit locale (default is 7-bit U.S. ASCII).

M *or* MULTILINE *or* (?m)
Matches to each newline, not whole string.

S *or* DOTALL *or* (?s)
. matches *all* characters, including newline.

U *or* UNICODE *or* (?u)
Makes \w, \W, \b, \B, \s, \S, \d, and \D dependent on Unicode character properties (new in Version 2.0).

X *or* VERBOSE *or* (?x)
Ignores whitespace in the pattern, outside character sets.

---

[*] A section on the prior regex module has been removed from this book; regex is now considered deprecated, and all new development should use the re module documented here for pattern matching.

`match(pattern, string [, flags])`

> If zero or more characters at start of string match the pattern string, returns a corresponding `MatchObject` instance, or `None` if no match. flags as in `compile`.

`search(pattern, string [, flags])`

> Scans through string for a location matching pattern; returns a corresponding `MatchObject` instance, or `None` if no match. flags as in `compile`.

`split(pattern, string [, maxsplit=0])`

> Splits string by occurrences of pattern. If capturing ( ) are used in pattern, occurrences of patterns or subpatterns are also returned.

`sub(pattern, repl, string [, count=0])`

> Returns string obtained by replacing the (first count) leftmost nonoverlapping occurrences of pattern (a string or an RE object) in string by repl. repl can be a string or a function called with a single `MatchObject` argument, which must return the replacement string. repl can also include sequence escapes \1, \2, etc., to use substrings that match groups, or \0 for all.

`subn(pattern, repl, string [, count=0])`

> Same as `sub`, but returns a tuple (new-string, number-of-subs-made).

`findall(pattern, string [, flags])`

> Returns a list of strings giving all nonoverlapping matches of pattern in string. If one or more groups are present in the pattern, returns a list of groups.

`finditer(pattern, string [, flags])`

> Returns an iterator over all nonoverlapping matches for the RE pattern in string (match objects).

`escape(string)`

> Returns string with all nonalphanumeric backslashed characters, such that they can be compiled as a string literal.

Regular Expression Objects

RE objects are returned by the re.compile function and have the following attributes.[*]

flags
> The flags argument used when the RE object was compiled.

groupindex
> Dictionary of {group-name: group-number} in the pattern.

pattern
> The pattern string from which the RE object was compiled.

```
match(string [, pos [, endpos]])
search(string [, pos [, endpos]])
split(string [, maxsplit=0])
sub(repl, string [, count=0])
subn(repl, string [, count=0])
findall(string [, pos[, endpos]])
finditer(string [, pos[, endpos]])
```
> Same as earlier re module functions, but pattern is implied, and pos and endpos give start/end string indexes for the match.

Match Objects

Match objects are returned by successful match and search operations, and have the following attributes (see the Python Library Reference for additional attributes omitted here).

pos, endpos
> Values of pos and endpos passed to search or match.

re
> RE object whose match or search produced this.

---

[*] In Version 1.6 and later, pattern and match objects are internal types, not PatternObject or MatchObject instances.

string

String passed to match or search.

group([g1, g2,...])

Returns substrings that were matched by parenthesized groups in the pattern. Accepts zero or more group numbers. If one argument, result is the substring that matched the group whose number is passed. If multiple arguments, result is a tuple with one matched substring per argument. If no arguments, returns entire matching substring. If any group number is 0, return value is entire matching string; otherwise, returns string matching corresponding parenthesized group number in pattern (1...N, from left to right). Group number arguments can also be group names.

groups()

Returns a tuple of all groups of the match; groups not participating in the match have a value of None.

groupdict()

Returns a dictionary containing all the named subgroups of the match, keyed by the subgroup name.

start([group]), end([group])

Indexes of start and end of substring matched by group (or entire matched string, if no group). If match object M, M.string[M.start(g):M.end(g)]==M.group(g).

span([group])

Returns the tuple (start(group), end(group)).

expand(template)

Returns the string obtained by doing backslash substitution on the template string template, as done by the sub method. Escapes such as \n are converted to the appropriate characters, and numeric back-references (\1, \2) and named back-references (\g<1>, \g<name>) are replaced by the corresponding group.

Pattern Syntax

Pattern strings are specified by concatenating forms (see Table 19) as well as by character class escapes (see Table 20). Python character escapes (e.g., \t for tab) can also appear. Pattern strings are matched against text strings, yielding a Boolean match result, as well as grouped substrings matched by subpatterns in parentheses:

```
>>> import re
>>> patt = re.compile('hello[ \t]*(.*)')
>>> mobj = patt.match('hello   world!')
>>> mobj.group(1)
'world!'
```

In Table 19, C is any character, R is any regular expression form in the left column of the table, and m and n are integers. Each form usually consumes as much of the string being matched as possible, except for the nongreedy forms (which consume as little as possible, as long as the entire pattern still matches the target string).

Table 19. Regular expression pattern syntax

Form	Description
.	Matches any character (including newline if DOTALL flag is specified).
^	Matches start of string (of every line in MULTILINE mode).
$	Matches end of string (of every line in MULTILINE mode).
C	Any nonspecial character matches itself.
R*	Zero or more occurrences of preceding regular expression R (as many as possible).
R+	One or more occurrences of preceding regular expression R (as many as possible).
R?	Zero or one occurrence of preceding regular expression R.
R{m,n}	Matches from m to n repetitions of preceding regular expression R.

Table 19. Regular expression pattern syntax (continued)

Form	Description
R*?, R+?, R??, R{m,n}?	Same as *, +, and ?, but matches as few characters/times as possible; *nongreedy*.
[...]	Defines character set; e.g., [a-zA-Z] matches all letters (also see Table 20).
[^...]	Defines complemented character set: matches if character is not in set.
\	Escapes special characters (e.g., *?+| ( )) and introduces special sequences (see Table 20). Due to Python rules, write as \\ or r'\\'.
\\	Matches a literal \; due to Python string rules, write as \\\\ in pattern, or r'\\'.
R|R	Alternative: matches left or right R.
RR	Concatenation: matches both Rs.
(R)	Matches any RE inside ( ), and delimits a group (retains matched substring).
(?: R)	Same as (R) but doesn't delimit a group.
(?= R)	Look-ahead assertion: matches if R matches next, but doesn't consume any of the string (e.g., X (?=Y) matches X if followed by Y).
(?! R)	Negative look-ahead assertion: matches if R doesn't match next. Negative of (?=R).
(?P<name> R)	Matches any RE inside ( ) and delimits a named group (e.g., r'(?P<id>[a-zA-Z_]\w*)' defines a group named id).
(?P=name)	Matches whatever text was matched by the earlier group named name.
(?<= R)	Positive look-behind assertion: matches if preceded by a match of fixed-width R.
(?<! R)	Negative look-behind assertion: matches if not preceded by a match of fixed-width R.
(?#...)	A comment; ignored.
(?letter)	letter is one of i, L, m, s, x, or u. Set flag (re.I, re.L, etc.) for entire RE.

In Table 20, \b, \B, \d, \D, \s, \S, \w, and \W behave differently depending on flags: if LOCALE (?L) is used, they depend on the current 8-bit locale; if UNICODE (?u) is used, they depend on the Unicode character properties; if neither flag is used, they assume 7-bit U.S. ASCII. Tip: use raw strings (r'\n') to literalize backslashes in Table 20 class escapes.

Table 20. Regular expression pattern special sequences

Sequence	Description
\num	Matches text of the group *num* (numbered from 1).
\A	Matches only at the start of the string.
\b	Empty string at word boundaries.
\B	Empty string not at word boundary.
\d	Any decimal digit (like [0-9]).
\D	Any nondecimal digit character (like [^0-9]).
\s	Any whitespace character (like [\t\n\r\f\v]).
\S	Any nonwhitespace character (like [^ \t\n\r\f\v]).
\w	Any alphanumeric character.
\W	Any nonalphanumeric character.
\Z	Matches only at the end of the string.

Object Persistence Modules

Three modules comprise the object persistence interface.

anydbm
>   Key-based string-only storage files.

pickle (and cPickle)
>   Serializes an in-memory object to/from file streams.

shelve
>   Key-based persistent object stores: pickles objects to/from anydbm files.

The shelve module implements persistent object stores. shelve in turn uses the pickle module to convert (serialize) in-memory Python objects to byte-stream strings and the anydbm module to store serialized byte-stream strings in access-by-key files.

anydbm and shelve Interfaces

DBM is an access-by-key filesystem: strings are stored and fetched by their string keys. The anydbm module selects the keyed-access file implementation in your Python interpreter and presents a dictionary-like API for scripts. A persistent object shelve is used like a simple *anydbm* file, except that the anydbm module is replaced by shelve, and the stored value can be almost any kind of Python object (but keys are still strings).

```
import shelve
import anydbm
```
   Gets dbm, gbmd, bsddb...whatever is installed.

```
file = shelve.open('filename')
file = anydbm.open('filename', 'c')
```
   Creates a new or opens an existing dbm file.

```
file['key1'] = value
```
   Store: creates or changes the entry for 'key1'.

```
value = file['key2']
```
   Fetch: loads the value for the 'key2' entry.

```
count = len(file)
```
   Size: returns the number of entries stored.

```
index = file.keys()
```
   Index: fetches the stored keys list (can use in a for).

```
found = file.has_key('key3')
```
   Query: sees if there's an entry for 'key3'.

```
del file['key4']
```
Delete: removes the entry for 'key4'.

```
file.close()
```
Manual close; required to flush updates to disk for some underlying DBM interfaces.

Notes

- dbm files and shelves work like dictionaries that must be opened before use; all mapping operations and some dictionary methods work.
- For dbm files and shelves, can also pass mode ('r', 'w', etc.) and protection (access-mode) parameters to open if desired (some DBM flavors require extra arguments).

pickle Interface

The pickle interface converts nearly arbitrary in-memory Python objects to/from serialized byte-streams. Byte-streams can be directed to any file-like object that has the expected read/write methods. Unpickling re-creates the original in-memory object (with the same value, but a new identity).

See also the cPickle module (coded in C for speed enhancement and automatically used by shelve, if present), and the makefile method of socket objects (for shipping serialized objects over networks), both in the Python Library Reference.

```
P = pickle.Pickler(fileobject)
```
Makes a new pickler, for saving to an output file object.

```
P.dump(object)
```
Writes an object onto the pickler's file/stream.

```
pickle.dump(object, fileobject)
```
Combination of the previous two: pickles object onto file.

```
U = pickle.Unpickler(fileobject)
```
Makes unpickler, for loading from input file object.

`object = U.load( )`
> Reads an object from the unpickler's file/stream.

`object = pickle.load(fileobject)`
> Combination of the previous two: unpickles object from file.

`string = pickle.dumps(object)`
> Returns pickled representation of object as a string.

`object = pickle.loads(string)`
> Reads an object from a character string instead of a file.

Notes

- `Pickler` and `Unpickler` are exported classes.

- `fileobject` is an open file object, or any object that implements file object attributes called by the interface. `Pickler` calls the file `write` method with a string argument. `Unpickler` calls the file `read` method with a byte-count and `readline` without arguments.

- In recent releases, the `Pickler` constructor and the module's `dump` and `dumps` functions have an additional argument, which used to be a flag named `bin` and is now an integer named `protocol`. For more efficient but still backward-compatible pickling, use 1 in this argument; for the most efficient (but incompatible with pre-2.3 `unpicklers`) pickling, use 2. Using -1 automatically uses the highest protocol supported (and this works in older versions as well).

Tkinter GUI Module and Tools

Tkinter is a portable graphical user interface (GUI) construction library shipped with Python as a standard library module. Tkinter provides an object-based interface to the open source Tk library and implements native look and feel for Python-coded GUIs on Windows, X-Windows, and Mac OS. It is portable, simple to use, well-documented, widely used, mature, and well-supported.

Tkinter Example

In Tkinter scripts, *widgets* are customizable classes (e.g., Button, Frame), *options* are keyword arguments (e.g., text="press"), and *composition* refers to object embedding, not pathnames (e.g., Label(Top,...)):

```
from Tkinter import *              # widgets, constants

def msg():                         # callback handler
    print 'hello stdout...'

top = Frame()                      # make a container
top.pack()
Label(top,  text="Hello world").pack(side=TOP)
widget = Button(top, text="press", command=msg)
widget.pack(side=BOTTOM)
top.mainloop()
```

Tkinter Core Widgets

Table 21 lists the primary widget classes in the Tkinter module. These are true Python classes that can be subclassed and embedded in other objects. To create a screen device, make an instance of the corresponding class, configure it, and arrange it with one of the geometry manager interface methods (e.g., Button(text='hello').pack()).

Table 21. Tkinter core widget classes

Widget class	Description
Label	Simple message area
Button	Simple labeled pushbutton widget
Frame	Container for attaching and arranging other widget objects
Toplevel, Tk	Top-level windows managed by the window manager
Message	Multiline text-display field (label)
Entry	Simple single-line text entry field
Checkbutton	Two-state button widget, used for multiple-choice selections
Radiobutton	Two-state button widget, used for single-choice selections

Table 21. Tkinter core widget classes (continued)

Widget class	Description
Scale	A slider widget with scalable positions
PhotoImage	Image object for placing full-color images on other widgets
BitmapImage	Image object for placing bitmap images on other widgets
Menu	Options associated with a Menubutton or top-level window
Menubutton	Button that opens a Menu of selectable options/submenus
Scrollbar	Bar for scrolling other widgets (e.g., Listbox, Canvas, Text)
Listbox	List of selection names
Text	Multiline text browse/edit widget, support for fonts, etc.
Canvas	Graphics drawing area: lines, circles, photos, text, etc.
OptionMenu	*Composite*: pull-down selection list
ScrolledText	*Composite*: text with attached Scrollbar
Dialog	*Old*: common dialog maker (see new common dialog calls in the next section)
PanedWindow	A multipane window interface
LabelFrame	A labeled frame widget
Spinbox	A multiple selection widget

Common Dialog Calls

Module tkMessageBox

```
showinfo(title=None, message=None, **options)
showwarning(title=None, message=None, **options)
showerror(title=None, message=None, **options)
askquestion(title=None, message=None, **options)
askokcancel(title=None, message=None, **options)
askyesno(title=None, message=None, **options)
askretrycancel(title=None, message=None, **options)
```

Module tkSimpleDialog

```
askinteger(title, prompt, **kw)
askfloat(title, prompt, **kw)
askstring(title, prompt, **kw)
```

Module tkColorChooser

```
askcolor(color = None, **options)
```

Module tkFileDialog

```
class Open
class SaveAs
class Directory
askopenfilename(**options)
asksaveasfilename(**options)
askopenfile(mode="r", **options)
asksaveasfile(mode="w", **options)
askdirectory(**options)
```

The common dialog call options are defaultextension (added to filename if not explicitly given), filetypes (sequence of (label, pattern) tuples), initialdir (initial directory, remembered by classes), initialfile (initial file), parent (window in which to place the dialog box), and title (dialog box title).

Additional Tkinter Classes and Tools

Table 22 lists some commonly used Tkinter interfaces and tools beyond the core widget class and standard dialog set.

Table 22. Additional Tkinter tools

Tool category	Available tools
Tkinter-linked variable classes	StringVar, IntVar, DoubleVar, BooleanVar
Geometry management methods	pack, grid, place, plus configuration options
Scheduled callbacks	Widget after, wait, and update methods; file I/O callbacks
Other Tkinter tools	Clipboard access; bind/Event low-level event processing; widget config options; modal dialog box support
Tkinter extensions (Vaults of Parnassus site)	*PMW*: more widgets; *PIL*: images; *Komodo* and *PythonWorks*: Tkinter GUI builder, etc.

Tcl/Tk-to-Python/Tkinter Mappings

Table 23 compares Python's Tkinter API to the base Tk library as exposed by the Tcl language. In Python's Tkinter, the Tk GUI interface differs from Tcl in the following ways.

Creation
> Widgets are created as class instance objects by calling a widget class.

Masters (parents)
> Parents are previously created objects, passed to widget class constructors.

Widget options
> Options are constructor or `config` keyword arguments, or indexed keys.

Operations
> Widget operations (actions) become Tkinter widget class object methods.

Callbacks
> Callback handlers are any callable object: function, method, `lambda`, class with `__call__` method, etc.

Extension
> Widgets are extended using Python class inheritance mechanisms.

Composition
> Interfaces are constructed by attaching objects, not by concatenating names.

Linked variables
> Variables associated with widgets are Tkinter class objects with methods.

Table 23. Tk-to-Tkinter mappings

Operation	Tcl/Tk	Python/Tkinter
Creation	frame .panel	panel = Frame()
Masters	button .panel.quit	quit = Button(panel)
Options	button .panel.go -fg black	go = Button(panel, fg='black')
Configure	.panel.go config -bg red	go.config(bg='red') go['bg'] = 'red'
Actions	.popup invoke	popup.invoke()
Packing	pack .panel -side left -fill x	panel.pack(side=LEFT, fill=X)

Internet Modules and Tools

This section summarizes Python's support for Internet scripting.

Commonly Used Library Modules

Following are some of the more commonly used modules in the Python Internet modules set. This is just a representative sample; see the Python Library Reference for a more complete list.

socket

Low-level network communications support (TCP/IP, UDP, etc.). Interfaces for sending and receiving data over BSD-style sockets: socket.socket() makes an object with socket call methods (e.g., object.bind()). Most protocol and server modules use this module internally.

select

Interfaces to Unix and Windows select function. Waits for activity on one of N files or sockets. Commonly used to multiplex among multiple streams, or to implement timeouts. Works only for sockets on Windows, not files.

cgi

Server-side CGI script support: cgi.FieldStorage parses the input stream; cgi.escape applies HTML escape conventions to output streams. To parse and access form information: after a CGI script calls form=cgi.FieldStorage(), form is a dictionary-like object with one entry per form field (e.g., form["name"].value is form field name text).

urllib, urllib2

Fetches web pages and server script outputs from their Internet addresses (URLs): urllib.urlopen(*url*) returns file with read methods; also urllib.urlretrieve(*remote, local*). Supports HTTP, FTP, gopher, and local file URLs. Also has tools for escaping URL text: urllib.quote_plus(*str*) does URL escapes for text inserted into HTML output streams.

ftplib

FTP (file transfer) protocol modules. *ftplib* provides interfaces for Internet file transfers in Python programs. After *ftp=ftplib.FTP*('sitename'), ftp has methods for login, changing directories, fetching/storing files and listings, etc. Supports binary and text transfers; works on any machine with Python and an Internet connection.

httplib, nntplib

HTTP (web) and NNTP (news) protocol modules.

poplib, imaplib, smtplib

POP, IMAP (mail fetch), and SMTP (mail send) protocol modules.

telnetlib, gopherlib

Telnet and gopher protocol modules.

htmllib, sgmllib, xmllib, xml package, HTMLParser

Parses web page contents (HTML, SGML, and XML documents). xml package new in Version 2.0; HTMLParser new in Version 2.2.

xmlrpclib

> XML-RPC remote method call protocol (new in Version 2.2).

email.*

> Parses and constructs email messages, with headers and attachments.

rfc822

> Parses email-style header lines.

xdrlib

> Encodes binary data portably (also see socket modules earlier in this list).

mhlib, mailbox

> Processes complex mail messages and mailboxes.

mimetools, mimify

> Handles MIME-style message bodies.

multifile

> Reads messages with multiple parts.

uu, binhex, base64, binascii, quopri

> Encodes and decodes binary (or other) data transmitted as text.

urlparse

> Parses URL string into components.

SocketServer

> Framework for general net servers.

BaseHTTPServer

> Basic HTTP server implementation.

SimpleHTTPServer, CGIHTTPServer

> Specific HTTP web server request handler modules.

rexec, Bastion

Restricted code execution mode. Support for restricted (trusted/safe) execution of program code, especially useful for Internet-related applications.

Table 24 lists some of these modules by protocol type.

Table 24. Selected Python Internet modules by protocol

Protocol	Common function	Port number	Python module
HTTP	Web pages	80	httplib, urllib, xmlrpclib
NNTP	Usenet news	119	nntplib
FTP data default	File transfers	20	ftplib, urllib
FTP control	File transfers	21	ftplib, urllib
SMTP	Sending email	25	smtplib
POP3	Fetching email	110	poplib
IMAP4	Fetching email	143	imaplib
Telnet	Command lines	23	telnetlib
Gopher	Document transfers	70	gopherlib, urllib

Other Built-in Modules

This section documents a handful of additional built-in modules. See the Python Library Reference for details on all built-ins and the Vaults of Parnassus and PyPI web sites (described in "Assorted Hints," later in this book) for third-party modules and tools.

The math Module

The math module exports C standard math library tools for use in Python. Table 25 lists this module's exports; see the Python Library Reference for more details. Also see the cmath module in the Python library for complex number tools and the *NumPy* system for advanced numeric work. frexp and modf return two-item tuples for a single argument.

Table 25. math module exports

pi	e	acos(*x*)	asin(*x*)
atan(*x*)	atan2(*x*,*y*)	ceil(*x*)	cos(*x*)
cosh(*x*)	exp(*x*)	fabs(*x*)	floor(*x*)
fmod(*x*,*y*)	frexp(*x*)	hypot(*x*,*y*)	ldexp(*x*,*y*)
log(*x*)	log10(*x*)	modf(*x*)	pow(*x*,*y*)
sin(*x*)	sinh(*x*)	sqrt(*x*)	tan(*x*)
tanh(*x*)			

The time Module

Following is a partial list of time module exports. See the Python Library Reference for more details.

clock()

> Returns the current CPU time as a floating-point number expressed in seconds (CPU time for process so far). Useful for benchmarking and timing code sections.

ctime(secs)

> Converts a time expressed in seconds since the epoch to a string representing local time (e.g., ctime(time())). As of Version 2.1, the argument is optional and defaults to the current time if omitted.

time()

> Returns a floating-point number representing UTC time in seconds since the epoch. On Unix, epoch is 1970.

sleep(secs)

> Suspends the process's execution for secs seconds. secs can be a float to represent fractions of seconds.

The datetime Module

Tools for subtracting dates, adding days to dates, and so on. See the Python Library Manual for details.

```
from datetime import date, timedelta
>>> date(2004, 12, 17) - date(2004, 11, 29)
datetime.timedelta(18)

>>> date(2004, 11, 29) + timedelta(18)
datetime.date(2004, 12, 17)
```

Threading Modules

Threads are lightweight processes that share global memory (i.e., lexical scopes and interpreter internals) and all run in parallel within the same process. Python thread modules work portably across platforms.

thread

> Python's basic thread interface module. Tools to start, stop, and synchronize functions run in parallel. To spawn a thread: thread.start_new_thread(function, argstuple). Function start_new is a synonym for start_new_thread. To synchronize threads, use thread locks: lock=thread.allocate_lock(); lock.acquire(); *update-objects*; lock.release().

threading

> Module threading builds upon thread, to provide threading-oriented classes: Thread, Condition, Semaphore, Lock, etc. Subclass Thread to overload run action method.

Queue

> A multiproducer, multiconsumer FIFO queue of objects implementation, especially useful for threaded applications (see the Python Library Reference). Locks get and put operations to synchronize access to data on the queue.

Binary Data Parsing

The struct module provides an interface for parsing and constructing packed binary data as strings. Commonly used in conjunction with the rb and wb binary-mode file open modes. See the Python Library Manual for format datatype and endian codes.

string = struct.pack(fmt, v1, v2, ...)
> Returns a string containing the values v1, v2, etc., packed according to the given format. The arguments must match the values required by the format exactly, and the format string can specify the endian format of the result.

tuple = struct.unpack(fmt, string)
> Unpack the string according to the given format.

struct.calcsize(fmt)
> Return size of the struct (and hence of the string) corresponding to the given format.

Following is an example showing how to pack and unpack data using struct:

```
>>> import struct
>>> data = struct.pack("4si", "spam", 123)
>>> data
'spam{\x00\x00\x00'
>>> x, y = struct.unpack("4si", data)
>>> x, y
('spam', 123)
```

Python Portable SQL Database API

Python's portable database API provides script portability between different vendor-specific SQL database packages. For each vendor, install the vendor-specific extension module, but write your scripts according to the portable database API. Your database scripts will largely continue working unchanged after migrating to a different underlying vendor package.

Note that database extension modules are not part of the Python standard library; they must be fetched and installed separately. See also the section "Object Persistence Modules," earlier in this book, for simpler alternatives.

API Usage Example

```
from dcoracle import connect
connobj = connect("user/password@system")
cursobj = connobj.cursor()

value1, value2 = 'developer', 39
query = 'SELECT name, shoesize FROM empl WHERE job = ? AND
    age = ?'
cursobj.execute(query, (value1, value2))

results = cursobj.fetchall()
for (name, size) in results:
    print name, size
```

Module Interface

This and the following sections provide a *partial* list of exports; see the full API specification at *http://www.python. org* for details omitted here.

connect(parameters...)
Constructor for connection objects; represents a connection to the database. Parameters are vendor-specific.

paramstyle
String giving type of parameter marker formatting (e.g., qmark = ? style).

Warning
Exception raised for important warnings such as data truncations.

Error
Exception that is the base class of all other error exceptions.

Connection Objects

Connection objects respond to the following methods.

close()
>   Closes the connection now (rather than when __del__ is called).

commit()
>   Commits any pending transactions to the database.

rollback()
>   Rolls database back to the start of any pending transaction; closing a connection without committing the changes first will cause an implicit rollback.

cursor()
>   Returns a new cursor object using the connection.

Cursor Objects

Cursor objects represent database cursors, used to manage the context of a fetch operation.

description
>   Sequence of seven-item sequences; each contains information describing one result column: (name, type_code, display_size, internal_size, precision, scale, null_ok).

rowcount
>   Specifies the number of rows that the last execute* produced (for DQL statements like select) or affected (for DML statements like update or insert).

callproc(procname [,parameters])
>   Calls a stored database procedure with the given name. The sequence of parameters must contain one entry for each argument that the procedure expects; result is returned as a modified copy of the inputs.

`close()`

> Closes the cursor now (rather than when `__del__` is called).

`execute(operation [,parameters])`

> Prepares and executes a database operation (query or command); parameters can be specified as a list of tuples to insert multiple rows in a single operation (but executemany is preferred).

`executemany(operation, seq_of_parameters)`

> Prepares a database operation (query or command) and executes it against all parameter sequences or mappings in sequence `seq_of_parameters`. Similar to multiple execute calls.

`fetchone()`

> Fetches the next row of a query result set, returning a single sequence, or None when no more data is available.

`fetchmany([size=cursor.arraysize])`

> Fetches the next set of rows of a query result, returning a sequence of sequences (e.g., a list of tuples). An empty sequence is returned when no more rows are available.

`fetchall()`

> Fetches all (remaining) rows of a query result, returning them as a sequence of sequences (e.g., a list of tuples).

Type Objects and Constructors

`Date(year,month,day)`

> Constructs an object holding a date value.

`Time(hour,minute,second)`

> Constructs an object holding a time value.

`None`

> SQL NULL values are represented by the Python None on input and output.

Python Idioms and Hints

This section lists common Python coding tricks and general usage hints. Consult the Python Library Reference and Python Language Reference (*http://www.python.org/doc/*) for further information on topics mentioned here.

Core Language Hints

- S[:] makes a top-level (shallow) copy of any sequence; copy.deepcopy(X) makes full copies; list(L) and D.copy() copy lists and dictionaries.

- L[:0]=[X,Y,Z] inserts items at front of list L.

- L[len(L):]=[X,Y,Z], L.extend([X,Y,Z]), and L += [X,Y,Z] all insert multiple items at the end of a list, in-place.

- L.append(X) and X=L.pop() can be used to implement in-place stack operations, where the end of the list is the top of the stack.

- Use for key in D.keys(): to iterate through dictionaries, or simply for key in D: in Version 2.2 and later.

- Use K=D.keys(); K.sort(); for key in K: to iterate over dictionary items in sorted fashion, or use the built-in sorted() function in Version 2.4 and later.

- X=A or B or None assigns X to the first true object among A and B, or None if both are false (i.e., 0 or empty).

- X,Y = Y,X swaps the values of X and Y.

- red, green, blue = range(3) assigns integer series.

- Use try/finally statements to ensure that termination code is run; especially useful around locking calls (acquire before the try, release in the finally).

Environment Hints

- Use `if __name__ == '__main__':` to add self-test code or a call to a main function at the bottom of module files; true only when file is run, not when it is imported as a library component.

- To load file contents in a single expression, use `bytes=open('filename').read()`.

- To iterate through text files, use `for line in file:` in Version 2.2 and later (in older versions, use `for line in file.readlines():`).

- To make a file an executable script on Unix-like platforms, add a line like `#!/usr/bin/env python` or `#!/usr/local/bin/python` at the top and give the file executable permissions with a `chmod` command. On Windows, file icons can be clicked.

- To retrieve command-line arguments, use `sys.argv`.

- To retrieve shell environment settings, use `os.environ`.

- The standard streams are: `sys.stdin`, `sys.stdout`, and `sys.stderror`.

- To return a list of files matching a given pattern, use: `glob.glob("pattern")`.

- To return a list of files and subdirectories on a path, use, for example: `os.listdir('.')`.

- To run shell commands within Python scripts, you can use `os.system("cmdline")`, `output=os.popen("cmdline", 'r').read()`, `os.popen2/3/4`, or `os.fork/execv`.

- The `dir([object])` function is useful for inspecting attribute namespaces; `print object.__doc__` often gives documentation.

- The `help([object])` function provides interactive help for modules, functions, types, and more; `help(str)` gives help on the `str` type; `help("`*`module`*`")` gives help on modules even if they have not yet been imported; and `help("`*`topic`*`")` gives help on keywords and other help topics (use `"topics"` for a list of help topics).

- `print` and `raw_input()` use `sys.stdout/stdin` streams: assign to file-like objects to redirect I/O internally (or use the `print >> file, text` statement format).

Usage Hints

- Use `from __future__ import` *`featurename`* to enable experimental language features that might break existing code.

- Intuition about performance in Python programs is usually wrong: always measure before optimizing or migrating to C. Use the `profile` and `time` modules.

- See modules `unittest` (a.k.a. PyUnit) and `doctest` for unit-testing tools shipped with the Python standard library; `unittest` is a class framework; `doctest` scans documentation strings for tests and outputs.

- See the `pydoc` library module and script shipped with Python for extraction and display of documentation strings associated with modules, functions, classes, and methods.

- See the section "Warnings Framework" in the "Built-in Exceptions" section, earlier in this book, as well as -W in the section "Command-line Options," earlier in this book, for details about turning off future-deprecation warnings emitted by the interpreter.

- See *Distutils*, *installer*, *py2exe*, *freeze*, and other tools for Python program distribution options.

- See *installer* and *py2exe* for turning Python programs into *.exe* files for Windows.

- See *NumPy* (and numarray) for extensions that turn Python into a numeric/scientific programming tool, with vector objects, etc.

- See *SWIG* (and others) for a tool that can automatically generate glue code for using C and C++ libraries within Python scripts.

- See *IDLE* for a development GUI shipped with Python, with syntax-coloring text editors, object browsers, debugging, etc.; see *PythonWin*, *Komodo*, *PythonWorks*, and others for additional IDE options.

- See *Emacs* help for tips on editing/running code in the Emacs text editor. Most other editors support Python as well (e.g., auto-indenting, coloring), including *VIM* and *IDLE*; see the editors page at *www.python.org*.

Assorted Hints

- Important web sites to refer to:

  http://www.python.org
  > The Python home page

  http://www.oreilly.com
  > The publisher's home page

  http://www.vex.net/parnassus
  > Third-party Python tool links

  http://www.python.org/pypi
  > Additional third-party Python tools

  http://www.rmi.net/~lutz
  > The author's site

- Python philosophy: import this.

- You should say spam and eggs instead of foo and bar in Python examples.

- Always look on the bright side of life.

Index

We'd like to hear your suggestions for improving our indexes. Send email to
index@oreilly.com.

X

Y

Z

Related Titles Available from O'Reilly

Scripting Languages

Exploring Expect

Jython Essentials

Learning PHP 5

Learning Python, *2nd Edition*

PHP Application Design Handbook

PHP Cookbook

PHP Pocket Reference, *2nd Edition*

PHP Security Handbook

Programming PHP, *2nd Edition*

Programming Python, *2nd Edition*

Python & XML

Python Cookbook

Python in a Nutshell

Python Standard Library

Ruby in a Nutshell

Upgrading to PHP 5

Web Database Applications with
PHP and MySQL, *2nd Edition*

Keep in touch with O'Reilly

1. Download examples from our books

To find example files for a book, go to:
www.oreilly.com/catalog

select the book, and follow the "Examples" link.

2. Register your O'Reilly books

Register your book at *register.oreilly.com*

Why register your books? Once you've registered your O'Reilly books you can:

- Win O'Reilly books, T-shirts or discount coupons in our monthly drawing.
- Get special offers available only to registered O'Reilly customers.
- Get catalogs announcing new books (US and UK only).
- Get email notification of new editions of the O'Reilly books you own.

3. Join our email lists

Sign up to get topic-specific email announcements of new books and conferences, special offers, and O'Reilly Network technology newsletters at:
elists.oreilly.com

It's easy to customize your free elists subscription so you'll get exactly the O'Reilly news you want.

4. Get the latest news, tips, and tools
www.oreilly.com

- "Top 100 Sites on the Web"—PC Magazine
- CIO Magazine's Web Business 50 Awards

Our web site contains a library of comprehensive product information (including book excerpts and tables of contents), downloadable software, background articles, interviews with technology leaders, links to relevant sites, book cover art, and more.

5. Work for O'Reilly

Check out our web site for current employment opportunities:
jobs.oreilly.com

6. Contact us

O'Reilly & Associates
1005 Gravenstein Hwy North
Sebastopol, CA 95472 USA

TEL: 707-827-7000 or 800-998-9938
(6am to 5pm PST)

FAX: 707-829-0104

order@oreilly.com
> For answers to problems regarding your order or our products.
> To place a book order online, visit:
> *www.oreilly.com/order_new*

catalog@oreilly.com
> To request a copy of our latest catalog.

booktech@oreilly.com
> For book content technical questions or corrections.

corporate@oreilly.com
> For educational, library, government, and corporate sales.

proposals@oreilly.com
> To submit new book proposals to our editors and product managers.

international@oreilly.com
> For information about our international distributors or translation queries. For a list of our distributors outside of North America check out:
> *international.oreilly.com/distributors.html*

adoption@oreilly.com
> For information about academic use of O'Reilly books, visit:
> *academic.oreilly.com*

O'REILLY®

Our books are available at most retail and online bookstores.
To order direct: 1-800-998-9938 • *order@oreilly.com* • *www.oreilly.com*
Online editions of most O'Reilly titles are available at *safari.oreilly.com*